VERSES *of* VIRTUE

VERSES *of* VIRTUE

THE POETRY AND PROSE OF CHRISTIAN WOMANHOOD

COMPILED AND EDITED BY
ELIZABETH BEALL PHILLIPS

"Who can find a virtuous woman?
for her price is far above rubies."
—*Proverbs 31:10*

THE VISION FORUM, INC.
San Antonio, Texas

To My Beloved Sons,
Joshua, Justice, and Honor

My fervent prayer is that God may send each of you godly, submissive, lovely, virtuous wives who are not ashamed to be called "mother," "wife," "helpmeet," and "keeper at home." I love you, my little men.

—Your Devoted Mother

CONTENTS

INTRODUCTION

A word fitly spoken is like apples of gold in pictures of silver.
Proverbs 25:11

Do you remember when, as a child, you stared at one object so long that your eyes crossed and the whole picture lost focus and became blurry? For many of us, the rush of details and obligations that make up a woman's life has the same effect—disorientation. Everything slips out of focus in our lives when we lose perspective. In fact, the Bible makes it clear that without a clear vision, we perish.

Poetry is one of God's ordained means for communicating vision and helping us to retain our focus as women of purpose and mission. This has been true from the beginning. The first words of love communicated of woman by man were poetic words of appreciation and understanding. Drawing upon the beauty of parallelism in expression, Adam declared of Eve: "This is now bone of my bones, and flesh of my flesh."

And so it goes throughout all the Scriptures. From the Psalms of David, to the poetry of Isaiah, to the verses of Deborah, to the songs of Solomon, and even the divinely inspired prose of John foretelling the return of the bridegroom, our Lord uses the beauty of language to motivate and to inspire. These are God's verses of virtue.

I am thankful that at each stage of my life, I was exposed not only to divinely inspired verses of virtue, but to prose and poetry that complemented the truths of Holy Scripture. Very precious to me are the three tiny palm-size books that sit behind glass in my room. They have brought me joy since I first read from them as a child. Though worn and yellowed with time, I still delight in their ancient words.

It was on the day of our engagement that my own dear husband gave me a special book of bridal poems containing the following verse:

> Oft, oft methinks, the while with Thee
> I breathe, as from the heart, thy dear
> And dedicated name, I hear
> A promise and a mystery,
> A pledge of more than passing life,
> Yea, in that very name of Wife!
> —Coleridge

Since those early days together, Doug and I have made it a point to collect and share poems with each other, and later with our children. Our home office is strewn with books of poetry and manila folders full of assorted scraps and fragments of verse. These books and scraps often find their way to our dinner table, where our family patriarch loves to regale the children with his favorite selections.

Eventually, this family tradition developed into a community affair, with special "poetry nights" at our home. A few friends, tea and cake, and cherished, inspiring poems have made for many, many happy evenings. From our youngest readers to the veteran bibliophiles, everyone comes prepared to read or recite a favorite selection. (One evening, a famous newspaper columnist joined us and was so exuberant in his delivery that he smashed the podium he was using.)

The following volume is humbly submitted to the reader in the hope that she will find an ample source of prosaic and poetic inspiration to last many such glorious evenings. More importantly, I have attempted to include selections designed to lift the heart of mothers and daughters alike, to offer them great encouragement for the journey of virtuous womanhood, and provide for them oft-ignored blessings on the glorious calling of wife and mother. In a world that minimizes motherhood, belittles the blessing of children, and frowns on femininity, it is our duty to fight back with parables of praise and verses of virtue.

VISIONS OF VIRTUE

Finally, brethren, whatsoever things are true,
whatsoever things are honest, whatsoever things are
just, whatsoever things are pure, whatsoever things are
lovely, whatsoever things are of good report; if there
be any virtue, and if there be any praise, think on
these things.

PHILIPPIANS 4:8

Who can find a virtuous woman? for her price is far
above rubies.

PROVERBS 31:10

A Vision of Virtue

Over the years, I have observed my husband praise my daughters and me publicly on many occasions, but he also does so in the privacy of our home. It is unusual for a week or even days to go by when he does not encourage my daughters by thanking them for helping mother, for dressing like ladies, or for helping with the baby. He talks to them about how wonderful it will be to grow up and become a mommy. He speaks to our sons about being protectors of women, and of the importance of "marrying a woman like Momma" someday.

By praising femininity, he hopes to give a vision of appreciation for virtuous womanhood to our sons and daughters. By communicating his honest gratitude for my role as his helpmeet, he hopes to provide each of them with an environment in which they know that Christian womanhood is highly esteemed, and with a pattern they can embrace in their own households someday.

Why is it important that we cast a vision for our children? Without a vision, they will perish. Without vision, they will despair for lack of hope. The vision of the world is dark and selfish. We must supplant it with the shining beauty of a vision of virtue.

The following works of prose and poetry remind us of and refresh our spirits in the reality that beautiful girlhood, virtuous motherhood, godly homemaking, purity, discretion, honor, industry, creativity, intelligence, and submission are all parts of the glorious vision of Christian womanhood.

The Virtuous Woman

Who can find a virtuous woman? for her price is far above rubies. The heart of her husband doth safely trust in her, so that he shall have no need of spoil. She will do him good and not evil all the days of her life.

She seeketh wool, and flax, and worketh willingly with her hands. She is like the merchants' ships; she bringeth her food from afar. She riseth also while it is yet night, and giveth meat to her household, and a portion to her maidens.

She considereth a field, and buyeth it: with the fruit of her hands she planteth a vineyard. She girdeth her loins with strength, and strengtheneth her arms. She perceiveth that her merchandise is good: her candle goeth not out by night. She layeth her hands to the spindle, and her hands hold the distaff. She stretcheth out her hand to the poor; yea, she reacheth forth her hands to the needy.

She is not afraid of the snow for her household: for all her household are clothed with scarlet. She maketh herself coverings of tapestry; her clothing is silk and purple.

Her husband is known in the gates, when he sitteth among the elders of the land.

She maketh fine linen, and selleth it; and delivereth girdles unto the merchant. Strength and honour are her clothing; and she shall rejoice in time to come.

She openeth her mouth with wisdom; and in her tongue is the law of kindness. She looketh well to the ways of her household, and eateth not the bread of idleness.

Her children arise up, and call her blessed; her husband also, and he praiseth her. Many daughters have done virtuously, but thou excellest them all.

Favour is deceitful, and beauty is vain: but a woman that feareth the LORD, she shall be praised. Give her of the fruit of her hands; and let her own works praise her in the gates.

Selections from Proverbs 31

➳

HOME: THE FOUNTAIN-HEAD OF SOCIETY

The household is the fountain-head of society. Both the commonwealth and the church grow out of the family. They both take their character from the family. The real seed-corn whence our republic sprang was the Christian households, which stepped forth from the cabin of the *Mayflower*, or which set up the family altar of the Hollander and the Huguenot on Manhattan Island or in the sunny South. All our best characters, best legislation, best institutions, and best church-life were cradled in those early homes. They were the tap-root of the republic, and of the American churches.

For one, I care but little for the government which presides at Washington in comparison with the government which rules the eight or ten millions of American homes. No administration can seriously harm us if our home-life is pure, frugal, and godly. No statesmanship or legislation can save us, if once our homes become the abodes of ignorance or the nestling-places of profligacy. The home rules the nation. If the home is demoralized it will ruin it.

There are several essentials to a good home. Wealth is not one of those essentials, for in many an abode of honest poverty contentment dwells. Out of such lowly cottages and cabins have sprung our greatest, noblest men and women. The little clapboarded farm houses of New England have been the nurseries of our greatest divines, most useful philanthropists and devoted missionaries. The riches of those humble dwellings were industrious hands and praying hearts. God's Word was the light of the homestead. The Bible, the spinning-wheel, and the family altar stood side by side. The growing refinements of later years have introduced into many rural habitations the piano, the pictures, and the pile of books. But let our people see to it that the increase of culture, money and refinement is not attended with any decrease of homespun frugality, domestic purity, and the fear of God.

A truly good home is not only one in which God reigns, but it must be an attractive spot. Even all the conscientious Christian parents do not seem to find this out. The result is that the theatre, the billiard-saloon, the club, the convivial party manage to "out-bid" the home, and to draw away the sons and the daughters. It is too often the fault of his parents, that a sprightly boy prefers some other evening resort to the stupid or disagreeable place in which he eats and sleeps. If his home were made more attractive he would not seek the haunts of danger and depravity. And one of the surest methods of keeping a husband out of a dram-shop, or a son out of the haunts of sin, is the "expulsive power of a new affection" for their home. Everything that attracts our children to their homes is very apt to be, in the end, an attraction towards Heaven.

Theodore Kuyler

ॐ

The Need of the Hour

What does out country need? Not armies standing
    With sabers gleaming ready for the fight;
Not increased navies, skillful and commanding,
    To bound the waters with an iron might;
Not haughty men with glutted purses trying
    To purchase souls, and keep the power of place;
Not jeweled dolls with one another vying
    For palms of beauty, elegance, and grace.

But we want women, strong of soul, yet lowly
    With that rare meekness, born of gentleness;
Women whose lives are pure and clean and holy,
    The women whom all little children bless;
Brave, earnest women, helpful to each other,
    With finest scorn for all things low and mean;
Women who hold the names of wife and mother
    Far nobler than the title of a queen.

Oh! These are they who mould the men of story,
    These mothers, ofttime shorn of grace and youth,
Who, worn and weary, ask no greater glory
    Than making some young soul the home of truth;
Who sow in hearts all fallow for the sowing
    The seeds of virtue and of scorn for sin,
And, patient, watch the beauteous harvest growing
    And weed out tares which crafty hands cast in.

Women who do not hold the gift of beauty
    As some rare treasure to be bought and sold,
But guard it as a precious aid to duty—
    The outer framing of the inner gold;
Women who, low above their cradles bending,
    Let flattery's voice go by, and give no heed,
While their pure prayers like incense are ascending
    These are our country's pride, our country's need.

Ella Wheeler Wilcox

࿐

PETER MARSHALL'S CHALLENGE

*Peter Marshall, one-time chaplain to the U.S. Senate, exhorting
American women, said the following:*

The modern challenge to motherhood is the eternal challenge—
that of being godly women. The very phrase sounds strange in our
ears. We never hear it now.

We hear about every other kind of women—beautiful women,
smart women, sophisticated women, career women, talented women,
divorced women.

But so seldom do we hear of a godly woman—or of a godly man
either, for that matter.

I believe women come nearer fulfilling their God-given function
in the home than anywhere else.

It is a much nobler thing to be a good wife than to be Miss
America.

It is a greater achievement to establish a Christian home than it is
to produce a second-rate novel, filled with filth.

It is a far, far better thing in the realms of morals to be old-
fashioned than to be ultra-modern.

The world has enough women who know how to hold their
cocktails, who have lost all their illusions and their faith.

The world has enough women who know how to be smart.

It needs women who are willing to be simple.

The world has enough women who know how to be brilliant.

It needs some who will be brave.

The world has enough women who are popular.

It needs more who are pure.

We need women, and men, too, who would rather be morally
right than socially correct.

Let us not fool ourselves—without Christianity, without Christian
education, without the principles of Christ inculcated into young life,
we are simply rearing pagans.

Physically, they will be perfect. Intellectually, they will be brilliant. But spiritually, they will be pagan. Let us not fool ourselves.

The twentieth century challenge to motherhood—when it is all boiled down—is that mothers will have an experience of God . . . a reality which they can pass on to their children.

Peter Marshall, Mr. Jones, Meet the Master

❧

The Secret of a Beautiful Life

There lived once a young girl whose perfect grace of character was the wonder of those who knew her. She wore on her neck a gold locket which no one was ever allowed to open. One day, in a moment of unusual confidence, one of her companions was allowed to touch its spring and learn its secret. She saw written these words—"Whom having not seen, I love." That was the secret of her beautiful life.

❧

9

HEARTH AND HOME

The aged women likewise, that they be in behaviour as becometh holiness, not false accusers, not given to much wine, teachers of good things; That they may teach the young women to be sober, to love their husbands, to love their children, To be discreet, chaste, keepers at home, good, obedient to their own husbands, that the word of God be not blasphemed. TITUS 2:3-5

Every wise woman buildeth her house: but the foolish plucketh it down with her hands. PROVERBS 14:1

She looketh well to the ways of her household, and eateth not the bread of idleness. PROVERBS 31:27

But if any widow have children or nephews, let them learn first to shew piety at home, and to requite their parents: for that is good and acceptable before God. . . . Let not a widow be taken into the number under threescore years old, having been the wife of one man. Well reported of for good works; if she have brought up children, if she have lodged strangers, if she have washed the saints' feet, if she have relieved the afflicted, if she have diligently followed every good work. But the younger widows refuse: for when they have begun to wax wanton against Christ, they will marry; Having damnation, because they have cast off their first faith. And withal they learn to be idle, wandering about from house to house; and not only idle, but tattlers also and busybodies, speaking things which they ought not. I will therefore that the younger women marry, bear children, guide the house, give none occasion to the adversary to speak reproachfully. SELECTIONS FROM 1 TIMOTHY 5

Hearth and Home

Home is the grandest of all institutions.
C.H. Spurgeon

Two of the most significant events of the twentieth century were women leaving the home *en masse* for corporate America, and the subsequent transformation of the home from a bastion of Christian family life, domesticity and culture; to a mere flop-house of individuals co-existing under one roof. For six thousand years, the home was the nerve center of society. Men fought and died on foreign battlefields—not just for abstract—but to secure the living, ever-present memory of blessed family life, typified by the phrase "hearth and home."

In the Scriptural model, we see the home as an incubator for leadership and dominion, as a grand instrument for education and discipleship, as the first expression of Godly culture, as a place of industry and economic self-sufficiency, as the primary outlet for hospitality and even evangelism—not to mention its significance as the first law-enforcing institution to which man is exposed on his journey from childhood to maturity.

It is to the mother—as the vice-regent of the home—that the responsibility is delegated by the husband for cultivating its aesthetic beauties and virtues. In the hands of noble womanhood, we can yet see—rising from the ashes of a broken culture—the glories of hearth and home, so that future generations will arise and declare its virtues once again.

13

Home Sweet Home ❧

HOME, SWEET HOME

'Mid pleasures and palaces though we may roam,
Be it ever so humble, there's no place like home;
A charm from the sky seems to hallow us there,
Which, seek through the world, is ne'er met with elsewhere.
 Home, home, sweet, sweet home!
There's no place like home, oh, there's no place like home!

An exile from home, splendor dazzles in vain;
Oh, give me my lowly thatched cottage again!
The birds singing gayly, that came at my call—
Give me them—and the peace of mind, dearer than all!
 Home, home, sweet, sweet home!
There's no place like home, oh, there's no place like home!

I gaze on the moon as I tread the drear wild,
And feel that my mother now thinks of her child,
As she looks on that moon from our own cottage door
Thro' the woodbine, whose fragrance shall cheer me no more.
 Home, home, sweet, sweet home!
There's no place like home, oh, there's no place like home!

How sweet 'tis to sit 'neath a fond father's smile,
And the caress of a mother to soothe and beguile!
Let others delight 'mid new pleasure to roam,
But give me, oh, give me, the pleasures of home,
 Home, home, sweet, sweet home!
There's no place like home, oh, there's no place like home!

To thee I'll return, overburdened with care;
The heart's dearest solace will smile on me there;
No more from that cottage again will I roam;
Be it ever so humble, there's no place like home.
    Home, home, sweet, sweet home!
There's no place like home, oh, there's no place like home!

John Howard Payne

THERE IS A LAND

There is a land of every land the pride,
Beloved by heaven o'er all the world beside;
Where brighter suns dispense serener light,
And milder moons emparadise the night;
A land of beauty, virtue, valor, truth,
Time-tutored age, and love-exalted youth.

The wandering mariner, whose eye explores
The wealthiest isles, the most enchanting shores,
Views not a realm so bountiful and fair,
Nor breathes the spirit of a purer air;
In every clime the magnet of his soul,
Touched by remembrance, trembles to that pole;
For in this land of heaven's peculiar grace,
The heritage of nature's noblest race,
There is a spot of earth supremely blest.
A dearer, sweeter spot than all the rest,
Where man, creation's tyrant, casts aside
His sword and scepter, pageantry and pride,
While in his softened looks benignly blend
The sire, the son, the husband, brother, friend.

15

Here woman reigns; the mother, daughter, wife,
Strew with fresh flowers the narrow way of life!
In the clear heaven of her delightful eye
An angel-guard of loves and graces lie;
Around her knees domestic duties meet,
And fireside pleasures gambol at her feet.
Where shall that land, that spot of earth be found?
Art thou a man?—a patriot?—look around;
Oh, thou shalt find, howe'er thy footsteps roam,
That land thy country, and that spot thy home.

James Montgomery

HOME

The dearest spot of earth to me
　　Is home, sweet home!
The fairy land I long to see
　　Is home, sweet home!
There how charmed the sense of hearing!
There where love is so endearing!
All the world is not so cheering
　　As home, sweet home!

I've taught my heart the way to prize
   My home, sweet home!
I've learned to look with lover's eyes
   On home, sweet home!
There, where vows are truly plighted!
There, where hearts are so united!
All the world besides I've slighted
   For home, sweet home.

W.T. Wrighton

ॐ

It Takes a Heap o' Livin'

It takes a heap o' livin' in a house t' make it home,
A heap o' sun an' shadder, an' ye sometimes have t' roam
Afore ye really 'preciate the things ye lef' behind,
An' hunger fer 'em somehow, with 'em allus on yer mind.
It don't make any differunce how rich ye get t' be,
How much yer chairs an' tables cost, how great yer luxury;
It ain't home t' ye, though it be the palace of a king,
Until somehow yer soul is sort o' wrapped round everything.

Home ain't a place that gold can buy or get up in a minute;
Afore it's home there's got t' be a heap o' livin' in it;
Within the walls there's got t' be some babies born, and then
Right there ye've got t' bring 'em up t' women good, an' men;
And gradjerly, as time goes on, ye find ye wouldn't part
With anything they ever used—they've grown into yer heart:
The old high chairs, the playthings, too, the little shoes they wore
Ye hoard; an' i ye could ye'd keep the thumb-marks on the door.

Ye've got t' weep t' make it home, ye've got t' sit an' sigh
An' watch beside a loved one's bed, an' know that Death is nigh;
An' in the stillness o' the night t' see Death's angel come.
An' close the eyes o' her that smiled, an' leave her sweet voice dumb.
For these are scenes that grip the heart, an' when yer tears are dried,
An' tuggin' at ye always are the pleasant memories
O' her that was an' is no more—ye can't escape from these.

Ye've got to sing an' dance fer years, ye've got t' romp an' play,
An' learn t' love the things ye have by usin' 'em each day;
Even the roses round the porch must blossom year by year
Afore they 'come a part o' ye, suggestin' someone dear
Who used t' love 'em long ago, and trained 'em just t' run
The way they do, so's they would get the early mornin' sun;
Ye've got to love each brick an' stone from cellar up t' dome:
It takes a heap o' livin' in a house t' make it home.

Edgar A. Guest

HOME DEFINED

Home's not merely four square walls,
　　Though with pictures bung and gilded:
Home is where affection calls,
　　Filled with shrines the heart hath builded!
Home! Go watch the faithful dove,
　　Sailing 'neath the heaven above us;
Home is where there's one to love!
　　Home is where there's one to love us!

Home's not merely roof and room,
　　It needs something to endear it;
Home is where the heart can bloom,
　　Where there's some kind lip to cheer it!
What is home with none to meet,
　　None to welcome, none to greet us?
Home is sweet,—and only sweet—
　　When there's one we love to meet us!

Charles Swain

Keeper at Home ᴖ

Women at Home

Thank God, O women, for the quietude of your home, and that you are queen in it. Men come at eventide to the home; but all day long you are there, beautifying it, sanctifying it, adorning it, blessing it. Better be there than wear a queen's coronet. Better be there than carry the purse of a princess. It may be a very humble home. There may be no carpet on the floor. There may be no pictures on the wall. There may be no silks in the wardrobe; but, by your faith in God, and your cheerful demeanor, you may garniture that place with more splendor than the upholsterer's hand ever kindled.

Rev. T. DeWitt Talmage, D.D.

ᴖ

THE HOME KEEPER

About her household moving glad each day,
  With heartfelt care of all the simplest things;
  And near her side a child's voice coos and sings;
She hears the noise of pattering feet at play,
And pauses oft to kiss the lips that say
  "Mother!" and joys to feel the hand that clings
  Close to her heart, as to her apron strings—
Nor would she chide that little hand away!
Then, when the day hath drifted to the dark,
  And brightening stars loom through the twilight late,
  She feels the heart within her bosom stir
At every leaf that strikes the lattice .... Hark!
  Her life's reward—a footstep at the gate,
  And love that comes to claim the love of her!

Frank L. Stanton

MRS. ROOSEVELT AT HOME

There are six children in the Roosevelt family, Alice, Theodore, Kermit, Ethel, Archibald and Quentin. Alice, who is seventeen, is the daughter of Mr. Roosevelt's first wife. The household has always been a very happy one. At Oyster Bay and in the Governor's Mansion at Albany, Mrs. Roosevelt has sought to preserve the simplicity and privacy of the typical, democratic American home. Father and mother were comrades for their children; the little folks were jolly as jolly could be; guests were welcomed with hearty hospitality. Appointments of the house were daintiness and comfort combined. Elaborate entertainments and "swell" dinners with gorgeous decorations were not chronicled of the Roosevelts. They are not rich, and they lived well within their means. At Oyster Bay, Mrs. Roosevelt was fond of going about in a walking-skirt, and playing with her children. She is brown-eyed, brown-haired and rosy. It is a cause of congratulation to all Americans that the beautiful home-life of the McKinleys will be followed by that of another pair of wedded lovers, whose devotion to each other has made marriage the blessed relation it should ever be. Mr. and Mrs. Roosevelt are the youngest couple who ever entered the White House; and with their troop of happy children they will make a merry place of the historic dwelling. The public will doubtless feel the same sort of affectionate interest and proprietorship in the little Roosevelts that they have extended to other White House children. Little folks of the Executive Mansion have always been regarded as the "nation's babies," so to speak.

From Mother, Home, and Heaven

❧

GOD GIVE US HOMES!

Homes where the Bible is honored and taught;
Homes with the Spirit of Christ in their thought;
Homes that a likeness to heaven have caught.
  God give us homes!

God give us homes!
Homes with the father in priest-like employ;
Homes that are bright with a far-reaching joy;
Homes where no world-stain shall come to annoy.
  God give us homes!

God give us homes!
Homes where the mother is queen-like in love;
Ruled in the fear of the Savior above;
Homes that to youth most inspiring shall prove.
    God give us homes!

God give us homes!
Homes with the children to brighten the hours;
Budding and blooming like beautiful flowers;
Places of sunshine—sweet, sanctified bowers.
    God give us homes!

By J.R. Clements

ॐ

GRATITUDE FOR HOME TRAINING

Our family life in Perth was a very united one; each evening, after the home-lessons were done, was given up to games of various kinds. We found our enjoyment and entertainment in our home; no outside amusements could possibly compare with the fun and happiness to be found there. We never had any desire to be out playing or walking with chums.. . .I feel traits in my character I knew not of before, and it causes me to bow in deeper gratitude for that home training which I have now left, for the training and disciplines of life. Oh! What a mighty influence home life has on us! Indeed, we do not know how deep a debt we owe to our mothers and fathers and their training.

Oswald Chambers

ॐ

A CHRISTIAN HOME

O give us homes built firm upon the Savior,
Where Christ is Head and Counselor and Guide;
Where every child is taught His love and favor
And gives his heart to Christ, the crucified:
How sweet to know that though his footsteps waver
His faithful Lord is walking by his side!

O give us homes with Godly fathers, mothers,
Who always place their hope and trust in Him:
Whose tender patience turmoil never bothers,
Whose calm and courage trouble cannot dim;
A home where each finds joy in serving others,
And love still shines, tho' days be dark and grim.

O Lord, our God, our homes are Thine forever!
We trust to Thee their problems, toil, and care;
Their bonds of love no enemy can sever
It Thou are always Lord and Master there:
Be Thou the center of our least endeavor—
Be Thou our Guest, our hearts and homes to share.

Barbara B. Hart

❧

GOD BLESS YOUR HOME

God bless your home
And all within,
The friends who come;
Your kith and kin;
Your shelt'ring roof,
Your homely fare,
Your place of rest,
Your toil and care.
Bless absent ones
And those you love,
And guard and guide
Them from above.
And grant that soon
Sweet peace will reign
In this and ev'ry land again.

Anonymous

Hospitality ❧

HOSPITALITY

Blest be that spot where cheerful guests retire
To pause from toil, and trim their evening fire;
Blest that abode, where want and pain repair,
And every stranger finds a ready chair:
Blest be those feasts with simple plenty crown'd,
Where all the ruddy family around
Laugh at the jest pity or pranks, that never fail,

Or sigh with pity at some mournful tale,
Or press the bashful stranger to his food,
And learn the luxury of doing good.

Oliver Goldsmith

ᕬ

Heart of Home

Lord, let our house be something more
Than just a shelter with a door;
    May its windows glow with light,
    Shedding radiance through the night.
Not just a glitter of glass and chrome,
But give it the "feel" of a happy home.

Let it have flowers, a well-loved book,
Soft cushions in a quiet nook.
    May it be more than downy bed,
    Or snowy cloth with silver spread;
Lend it some smiles, warm sympathy,
With kindly thought, true charity—
    That all may recall, though far they roam,
    That God was there—in the heart of home

Christine White

ᕬ

HARVEST HOME

Come, ye thankful people, come,
Raise the song of Harvest—come!
All is safely gathered in,
Ere the winter storms begin;
God, our Maker, doth provide
For our wants to be supplied;
Come to God's own temple, come;
Raise the song of Harvest-home!

What is earth but God's own field,
Fruit unto his praise to yield?
Wheat and tares therein are sown,
Unto joy or sorrow grown;
Ripening with a wondrous power,
Till the final Harvest-hour;
Grant, O Lord of life, that we
Holy grain and pure may be.

Come, then, Lord of Mercy, come,
Bid us sing the Harvest-home!
Let thy saints be gathered in!
Free from sorrow, free from sin;
All upon the golden floor
Praising thee forevermore;
Come, with thousand angels, come;
Bid us sing thy Harvest-home.

Henry Alford

❧

The Happiest Spot on Earth

The Christian home should be the happiest spot on earth, not only to the "grown ups" but to every member of the family. Let us see that we make it so even to the youngest. Never mind if they do make a noise and tumble the house about with their innocent games, and shout choruses when some of us older ones are trying to write articles in the next room. Thousands upon thousands of young people have gone to utter destruction for the reason that having cold, dull, stiff firesides at home they sought amusement elsewhere. How many sad parents today would give the world to hear the noisy steps of long-absent children. They would not mind how much the house was turned upside down, nor how dirty the carpets became, if only they could hear once more the cheery voice and feel the clinging arms about their necks and the warm cheeks laid upon theirs! So let us keep them at home by making home the very loveliest place on earth to them, the place of all others where god is honored, and where the whole atmosphere is filled with love and joy and peace.

Reader Harris

ॐ

THE BRIDE

*For as a young man marrieth a virgin, so shall thy
sons marry thee: and as the bridegroom rejoiceth over
the bride, so shall thy God rejoice over thee.*

ISAIAH 62:5

*The voice of joy, and the voice of gladness, the voice of
the bridegroom, and the voice of the bride, the voice
of them that shall say, Praise the LORD of hosts: for
the LORD is good; for his mercy endureth for ever:
and of them that shall bring the sacrifice of praise into
the house of the LORD. For I will cause to return the
captivity of the land, as at the first, saith the LORD.*

JEREMIAH 33:11

*Let thy fountain be blessed: and rejoice with the wife
of thy youth.*

PROVERBS 5:18

*Whoso findeth a wife findeth a good thing, and
obtaineth favour of the LORD.*

PROVERBS 18:22

*And did not he make one? Yet had he the residue of the
spirit. And wherefore one? That he might seek a godly
seed. Therefore take heed to your spirit, and let none
deal treacherously against the wife of his youth.*

MALACHI 2:15

*Thy wife shall be as a fruitful vine by the sides of
thine house: thy children like olive plants round about
thy table.*

PSALM 128:3

THE BRIDE

Since the day we were wed, my husband has referred to me as his "beloved bride." This term of endearment ever reminds me of the preciousness of the sacred gift of oneness God has given called marriage. I am his "bride." As Eve was given to Adam, so God gave me to him. As the church prepares for the Lord Jesus, so I was prepared for my husband.

After creation, marriage was God's first gift to man and woman. It remains God's precious gift, capped by the new life that flows from the union of man and woman. Even in a modern world of no-fault divorce, infidelity, and role-reversals, marriage can and must remain for the Christian the truest picture of the eternal and sacred love of Jesus Christ, the bridegroom, for His bride.

To be a bride is to be a living symbol of purity, of holy desire, and of completion. She is "the beloved" to her groom, and is to be cherished, protected, and loved. Through marriage the bride and the groom become the most potent force on earth for the advancement of the Church. They become a family, the truest incubator for Gospel evangelism, societal transformation, and dominion over the earth.

The world mocks marriage. Not so the Christian. We praise it, rejoice in it, and seek every opportunity to freely extol the virtues of this sacred gift in poetry and song.

Betrothal and Marriage ❧

LETTER TO A SUITOR

Before I trust my fate to thee,
Or place my hand in thine;
Before I let thy future give
Color and form to mine;
Before I peril all for thee,
Question thy soul tonight for me.

I break all slighter bonds, nor feel
A shadow of regret;
Is there one link within the past
That holds thy spirit yet?
Or is thy faith as clear and free
As that which I can pledge to thee?

Does there within thy dimmest dreams
A possible future shine,
Wherein thy life could henceforth breathe,
Untouched, unshared by mine?
If so, at any pain or cost,
Oh, tell me before all is lost.

Look deeper still. If thou canst feel
Within thy inmost soul
That thou hast kept a portion back,
While I have staked the whole,
Let no false pity spare the blow,
But in true mercy tell me so.

Is there within thy heart a need
That mine cannot fulfill?
One chord that any other hand
Could better wake or still?
Speak now—lest at some future day
My whole life wither and decay.

Lives there within thy nature bid
The demon-spirit Change,
Shedding a passing glory still
On all things new and strange?
It may not be thy fault alone—
But shield my heart against thine own.

Couldst thou withdraw thy hand one day
And answer to my claim
That Fate, and that to-day's mistake—
Not thou—had been to blame?
Some soothe their conscience thus; but thou
Wilt surely warn and save me now.

Miss Procter

❧

Song of Solomon

Behold, thou art fair, my love; behold, thou art fair; thou hast doves' eyes within thy locks: thy hair is as a flock of goats, that appear from mount Gilead. Thy teeth are like a flock of sheep that are even shorn, which came up from the washing; whereof every one bear twins, and none is barren among them. Thy lips are like a thread of scarlet, and thy speech is comely: thy temples are like a piece of a pomegranate within thy locks. Thy neck is like the tower of David builded for an armoury, whereon there hang a thousand bucklers, all shields of mighty men. . . . Until the day break, and the shadows flee away, I will get me to the mountain of myrrh, and to the hill of frankincense. Thou art all fair, my love; there is no spot in thee. Come with me from Lebanon, my spouse, with me from Lebanon: look from the top of Amana, from the top of Shenir and Hermon, from the lions' dens, from the mountains of the leopards. Thou hast ravished my heart, my sister, my spouse; thou hast ravished my heart with one of thine eyes, with one chain of thy neck. How fair is thy love, my sister, my spouse! how much better is thy love than wine! and the smell of thine ointments than all spices!

The First Words of Eve

O, thou for whom
And from whom I was formed flesh of thy flesh,
And without whom am to no end, my guide
And head!

Paradise Lost, *Book IV*

Biblical Wedding Blessings

And they blessed Rebekah, and said unto her: Thou art our sister, be thou the mother of thousands of millions, and let thy seed possess the gate of those which hate them.

Genesis 24:60

And all the people that were in the gate, and the elders, said: We are
witnesses!

The LORD make the woman that is come into thine house like
Rachel and like Leah, which two did build the house of Israel: and do
thou worthily in Ephratah, and be famous in Bethlehem.

Ruth 4:11

Gather the people, sanctify the congregation, assemble the elders,
gather the children, and those that suck the breasts: let the
bridegroom go forth of his chamber, and the bride out of her closet.

Joel 2:16

Made for Each Other ❧

WEDDED LIFE

Grow old along with me
the best is yet to be.

Robert Browning

❧

A GOOD WIFE

A good wife is Heaven's last, best gift to man, his angel and minister of
graces innumerable, his gem of many virtues; her voice his sweetest
music, her smiles his brightest day, her kiss the guardian of his innocence,
her arms the pale of his safety, the balm of his health, the sure balsam of

his life; her industry his surest wealth, her economy his safest steward, her lips his faithful counselor, her bosom the softest pillow of his cares, and her prayers the ablest advocate of Heaven's blessing on his head.

Anonymous Husband

As Unto the Bow

As unto the bow the cord is,
　　So unto the man is woman:
Though she bends him, she obeys him;
Though she draws him, yet she follows;
　　Useless each without the other.

Henry Wadworth Longfellow

My Wife

Trusty, dusky, vivid, true,
With eyes of gold and bramble-dew,
Steel true and blade-straight,
The great artificer
Made my mate.

Honour, anger, valour, fire;
A love that life could never tire,
Death quench or evil stir,
The mighty master
Gave to her.

36

Teacher, tender, comrade, wife,
A fellow-farer true through life,
Heart-whole and soul-free
The august father
Gave to me.

Robert Louis Stevenson

❧

To My Dear and Loving Husband

My head, my heart, mine Eyes, my life, nay more,
My joy, my Magazine of earthly store. . . .
If ever two were one, then surely we.
If ever man were lov'd by wife, then thee;
If ever wife was happy in a man,
Compare with me ye women if you can.
I prize thy love more then whole Mines of gold,
Or all the riches that the East doth hold.
My love is such that Rivers cannot quench,
Nor ought but love from thee, give recompense.
Thy love is such I can no way repay
The heavens reward thee manifold I pray.
Then while we live, in love lets so persevere,
That when we live no more, we may live ever.

Anne Bradstreet

❧

The Happy Husband

Oft, oft methinks, the while with thee,
   I breathe, as from the heart, thy dear
   And dedicated name, I hear
A promise and a mystery,
   A pledge of more than passing life,
   Yea, in that very name of Wife!

A pulse of love, that ne'er can sleep!
   A feeling that upbraids the heart
   With happiness beyond desert,
That gladness half requests to weep!
   Nor bless I not the keener sense
   And unalarming turbulence

Of transient joys, that ask no sting
   From jealous fears, or boy denying;
   But born beneath Love's brooding wing,
And into tenderness soon dying,
   Wheel out their giddy moment, then
   Resign the soul to love again;—

A more precipitated vein
   Of notes, that eddy in the flow
   Of smoothest song, they come, they go,
And leave their sweeter understrain,
   Its own sweet self—a love of Thee
   That seems, yet cannot greater be!

Samuel Taylor Coleridge

❧

YESTERDAYS WITH YOU

Today is blest, indeed—
Yet it is but a day;
I, with my friendly greed,
Hide memories away.
And that is why I say
I would old times were new,
Then I would trade Today
For Yesterdays with you.

Old friend, the dreams we had!
The songs we loved to hear!
Half gaily and half sad
Today they linger near.
Wherever I may go,
Whatever I may do,
They have a luring glow—
Those Yesterdays with you.

The waking world at dawn,
When glory pearled the skies—
The roads that lured us on
With goals that charmed our eyes;
The twilight with its hush
When bird calls faltered through—
What recollections rush
From Yesterdays with you!

Tomorrows reach away,
The world is very wide,
The Task-man of Today
Will never be denied,
But in the ruck and stress
Their skies gleam ever blue,
They quiet me, and bless—
My yesterdays with you.

With memory's magic art
I make Time thread its way
Down highways of the heart
To each fair yesterday—
And that is why I pray
Old times may be made new,
For I would trade Today
For Yesterdays with you.

Wilbur D. Nesbit

Americana ⁓

EVANGELINE

On the banks of the Têche, are the towns of St. Maur and St. Martin.
There the long-wandering bride shall be given again to her bridegroom,
There the long-absent pastor regain his flock and his sheepfold.
Beautiful is the land, with its prairies and forests of fruit trees;
Under the feet a garden of flowers, and the bluest of heavens

Bending above, and resting its dome on the walls of the forest.
They who dwell there have named it the Eden of Louisiana!

Henry Wadsworth Longfellow

⚶

THE WEDDING OF PRISCILLA

Forth from the curtain of clouds, from the tent of purple and scarlet,
Issued the sun, the great High-Priest, in his garments resplendent,
Holiness unto the Lord, in letters of light, on his forehead,
Round the hem of his robe the golden bells and pomegranates.
Blessing the world he came, and the bars of vapor beneath him
Gleamed like a grate of brass, and the sea at his feet was a laver!
This was the wedding morn of Priscilla the Puritan maiden.
Friends were assembled together; the Elder and Magistrate also
Graced the scene with their presence, and stood like the Law and the Gospel,
One with the sanction of earth and one with the blessing of heaven.
Simple and brief was the wedding, as that of Ruth and of Boaz.
Softly the youth and the maiden repeated the words of betrothal,
Taking each other for husband and wife in the Magistrate's presence,
After the Puritan way, and the laudable custom of Holland.
Fervently then, and devoutly, the excellent Elder of Plymouth
Prayed for the hearth and the home, that were founded that day in affection,
Speaking of life and of death, and imploring Divine benedictions.

Lo! when the service was ended, a form appeared on the threshold,
Clad in armor of steel, a sombre and sorrowful figure!
Why does the bridegroom start and stare at the strange apparition?
Why does the bride turn pale, and hide her face on his shoulder?
Is it a phantom of air,—a bodiless, spectral illusion?
Is it a ghost from the grave, that has come to forbid the betrothal?
Long had it stood there unseen, a guest uninvited, unwelcomed;

41

Over its clouded eyes there had passed at times an expression
Softening the gloom and revealing the warm heart hidden beneath them,
As when across the sky the driving rack of the rain-cloud
Grows for a moment thin, and betrays the sun by its brightness.
Once it had lifted its hand, and moved its lips, but was silent,
As if an iron will had mastered the fleeting intention.
But when were ended the troth and the prayer and the last benediction,
Into the room it strode, and the people beheld with amazement
Bodily there in his armor Miles Standish, the Captain of Plymouth!
Grasping the bridegroom's hand, he said with emotion, "Forgive me!
I have been angry and hurt,—too long have I cherished the feeling;
I have been cruel and hard, but now, thank God! it is ended.
Mine is the same hot blood that leaped in the veins of Hugh Standish,
Sensitive, swift to resent, but as swift in atoning for error.
Never so much as now was Miles Standish the friend of John Alden."
Thereupon answered the bridegroom: "Let all be forgotten between us,—
All save the dear old friendship, and that shall grow older and dearer!"
Then the Captain advanced, and bowing, saluted Priscilla,
Gravely, and after the manner of old-fashioned gentry in England,
Something of camp and of court, of town and of country, commingled,
Wishing her joy of her wedding, and loudly lauding her husband.
Then he said with a smile: "I should have remembered the adage,—
If you would be well served, you must serve yourself; and moreover,
No man can gather cherries in Kent at the season of Christmas!"

Great was the people's amazement, and greater yet their rejoicing,
Thus to behold once more the sunburnt face of their Captain,
Whom they had mourned as dead; and they gathered and crowded about him,
Eager to see him and hear him, forgetful of bride and of bridegroom,
Questioning, answering, laughing, and each interrupting the other,
Till the good Captain declared, being quite overpowered and bewildered,
He had rather by far break into an Indian encampment,
Than come again to a wedding to which he had not been invited.

Meanwhile the bridegroom went forth and stood with the bride at the doorway,
Breathing the perfumed air of that warm and beautiful morning.
Touched with autumnal tints, but lonely and sad in the sunshine.
Lay extended before them the land of toil and privation;
There were the graves of the dead, and the barren waste of the sea-shore,
There the familiar fields, the groves of pine, and the meadows;
But to their eyes transfigured, it seemed as the Garden of Eden,
Filled with the presence of God, whose voice was the sound of the ocean.

Soon was their vision disturbed by the noise and stir of departure,
Friends coming forth from the house, and impatient of longer delaying,
Each with his plan for the day, and the work that was left uncompleted.
Then from a stall near at hand, amid exclamations of wonder,
Alden the thoughtful, the careful, so happy, so proud of Priscilla,
Brought out his snow-white bull, obeying the hand of its master,
Led by a cord that was tied to an iron ring in its nostrils,
Covered with crimson cloth, and a cushion placed for a saddle.
She should not walk, he said, through the dust and heat of the noonday;
Nay, she should ride like a queen, not plod along like a peasant.
Somewhat alarmed at first, but reassured by the others,
Placing her hand on the cushion, her foot in the hand of her husband,
Gayly, with joyous laugh, Priscilla mounted her palfrey.
"Nothing is wanting now," he said with a smile, "but the distaff;
Then you would be in truth my queen, my beautiful Bertha!"

Onward the bridal procession now moved to their new habitation,
Happy husband and wife, and friends conversing together.
Pleasantly murmured the brook, as they crossed the ford in the forest,
Pleased with the image that passed, like a dream of love, through its bosom,
Tremulous, floating in air, o'er the depths of the azure abysses.
Down through the golden leaves the sun was pouring his splendors,
Gleaming on purple grapes, that, from branches above them suspended,
Mingled their odorous breath with the balm of the pine and the fir-tree,
Wild and sweet as the clusters that grew in the valley of Esheol.

Like a picture it seemed of the primitive, pastoral ages,
Fresh with the youth of the world, and recalling Rebecca and Isaac,
Old and yet ever new, and simple and beautiful always,
Love immortal and young in the endless succession of lovers.
So through the Plymouth woods passed onward the bridal procession.

From "The Courtship of Miles Standish"
by Henry Wadsworth Longfellow

Blessed Motherhood

The words of king Lemuel, the prophecy that his mother taught him. What, my son? and what, the son of my womb? and what, the son of my vows?

PROVERBS 31

A child left to himself bringeth his mother to shame.

PROVERBS 29:15

A wise son maketh a glad father.

PROVERBS 10:1

In like manner also, that women adorn themselves in modest apparel, with shamefacedness and sobriety; not with broided hair, or gold, or pearls, or costly array; But (which becometh women professing godliness) with good works. Let the woman learn in silence with all subjection. But I suffer not a woman to teach, nor to usurp authority over the man, but to be in silence. For Adam was first formed, then Eve. And Adam was not deceived, but the woman being deceived was in the transgression. Notwithstanding she shall be saved in childbearing, if they continue in faith and charity and holiness with sobriety.

1 TIMOTHY 2

MOTHERHOOD

At the time of this writing, God has allowed me the joy of bringing six new lives into the world—six lives! Each one is precious and unique. Each one is created in the image of God, and with a potential to change the world. They are my joy, my happiness, and daily delight. I can only pray that He will send many more. That he created me a woman, and allowed me to carry my children and deliver them into the world is truly extraordinary. What a trust He has given to women. What an honor. Shame on those of our sex who mock, belittle, and complain about motherhood.

You see, there is no higher calling, no greater privilege than being a vessel of life and later a teacher to souls which will live forever. This is a crucial point: These children will live forever, either in Heaven, or in Hell. We not only have the privilege of introducing them to the world, but God has given us the honor of assisting our husbands in the great work of introducing these little ones to the God who loves them. No empire, no credential, no golden treasure, no corporate success story can ever rival the glory of this calling.

Praying mothers, teaching mothers, faithful mothers—the Church needs you. She needs mothers who will crave children, and love them and bless them and train them to be the warriors of the next generation.

Motherhood! Blessed motherhood! The time has come to once again sing the praises of this calling. Though bloodied by the barbs of feminism, Christian motherhood will not be vanquished.

Visions of Motherhood ❧

MOTHER, HOME, AND HEAVEN

There are three words that sweetly blend,
  That on the heart are graven;
A precious soothing balm they lend—
  They're Mother, Home, and Heaven!

They twine a wreath of beauteous flowers,
  Which, placed on memory's urn,
Will e'en the longest, gloomiest hours
  To golden sunlight turn!

They form a chain whose every link
  Is free from base alloy;
A stream where whosoever drinks
  Will find refreshing joy!

They build an altar where each day
  Love's offering is renewed;
And peace illumes with genial ray
  Life's darkened solitude!

If from our side the first has fled,
  And Home be but a name,
Let's strive the narrow path to tread,
  That we the last may gain!

❧

YOUR HIGH CALLING

Mother, whoever you may be,
You may think long and earnestly
Of your high calling. Pondering
The undreamed honour of the thing;
Learning how God, through you, would plan
To be well known to every man.
And through your arms would gather fast
The whole world to His heart at last.

Fay Inchfawn

ം

THE TWO MOTHERS

A lady was calling upon a friend whose two children were brought in during the call. As they talked together the caller said eagerly, and yet with evidently no thought of the meaning of her words, "Oh, I'd give my life to have two such children." And the mother replied with a subdued earnestness whose quiet told of the depth of experience out of which her words came, "That's exactly what it costs!"

ം

THREE MOTHERS

Once a woman came upon three mothers at work. "What are you doing?' she asked of them.

"I'm doing the weekly washing," answered the first.

"I'm doing a bit of household drudgery," replied the second.

"I'm mothering three young children who someday will fill important and useful spheres in life, and wash-day is a part of my

grand task in caring for these souls who shall live forever," replied the
third. Only she had caught the vision of the great work she was doing.

New Life ᔰ

THE BABY

Another little wave
   Upon the sea of life;
Another soul to save,
   Amid the toil and strife.
Two more little feet
   To walk the dusty road;
To choose where two paths meet,
   The narrow and the broad.

Two more little hands,
   To work for good or ill;
Two more little eyes;
   Another little will;
Another heart to love,
   Receiving love again;
And so the baby came,
   A thing of joy and pain.

Providence Journal

ᔰ

SOMETIMES

Last night, my darling, as you slept,
I thought I heard you sigh,
And to your little crib I crept,
And watched a space thereby.
Then bending down I kissed your brow,
For oh! I love you so.
You are too young to know it now,
But sometime you shall know.

Eugene Field

THE NEW BABY

Here is a sweet, fragrant mouth to kiss; here are two more feet to make music with their pattering about my nursery. Here is a soul to train for God, and the body in which it dwells is worth all it will cost, since it is the abode of a kingly tenant. I may see less of friends, but I have gained one dearer than them all, to whom, while I minister in Christ's name, I make a willing sacrifice of what little leisure for my own recreation, my other darlings had left me. Yes, my precious baby, you are welcome to your mother's heart, welcome to her time, her strength, her health, her life-long prayers!

Elizabeth Stuart Phelps

MOTHERHOOD

I hold within my arms to-day
A priceless bit of mortal clay,
Divinely fashioned, and so fair,
The angels well may kinship share.

My soul with gratitude is filled,
My heart with mother love is thrilled,
My eyes brim o'er with new-born joy,
While gazing on my cherub boy.

O precious one! Through tears I see
A mighty task awaiting me.
My happy sky grows overcast,
Life's duties loom so grand, so vast.

To shield from wrong, to right incline,
This little life now linked to mine—
Divine the gift. Oh, may the mould
A heart of truth and honor hold!

Help me, kind Heaven, to know the way
From out the tangle of each day,
To guide him safe to manhood's prime,
And all the glory shall be Thine.

M.E. Piatt

❧

Mother's "Inspiration"

Had I no little feet to guide
   Along life's toilsome way,
My own more frequently might slide,
   More often go astray.

But when I meet my baby's eyes,
   At God's own bar I stand,
And angels draw me t'ward the skies
   While baby holds my hand.

McMaster

❧

He Has Lost His Baby Ways

Not long, alas! Not long; the mother-heart
Knows well how quickly she will have to part
With all this wonder; she who tries each art
To lure him on; the first to coax and praise
Each added grace; then first in sore amaze
To mourn that he has lost his baby ways!

Alice Wellington Rollins

❧

IN MEMORY OF MY DEAR GRAND-CHILD ELIZABETH BRADSTREET,
WHO DECEASED AUGUST, 1665 BEING A YEAR AND HALF OLD.

Farewel dear babe, my hearts too much content,
Farewel sweet babe, the pleasure of mine eye,
Farewel fair flower that for a space was lent,
Then ta'en away unto Eternity.
Blest babe why should I once bewail thy fate,
Or sigh the dayes so soon were terminate;
Sith thou art settled in an Everlasting state.

By Nature Trees do rot when they are grown.
And Plumbs and Apples thoroughly ripe do fall,
And Corn and grass are in their season mown,
And time brings down what is both strong and tall.
But plants new set to be eradicate,
And buds new blown, to have so short a date,
Is by his hand alone that guides nature and fate.

Anne Bradstreet

Devoted Mothers ❧

MOTHER, MOTHER, WATCH AND PRAY

Mother! Mother! Watch and pray,
Fling not golden hours away!
   Now or never, plant and sow,
   Catch the morning's earliest glow.

Mother! Mother! Guard the dew,
While it sparkles clear and true.
    No delay! The scorching noon
    May thy treasures reach too soon.

Mother! Point them to the sky,
Tell them of a loving eye,
    That more tender is than thine,
    And doth ever on them shine.

Mother! Lead them soon and late
To behold the golden gate;
    When they long to enter there,
    Lead them to the Lamb by prayer.

Mother, seize the precious hours,
While the dew is on thy flowers!
    Life is such a fleeting thing,
    Mother! Mother! Sow in spring.

Selected

ॐ

MOTHERS OF YOUNG CHILDREN

Oh, Mothers of young children, I bow before you in reverence. Your work is most holy. You are fashioning the destinies of immortal souls. The powers folded up in the little ones that you hushed to sleep in your bosoms last night, are powers that shall exist for ever. You are preparing them for their immortal destiny and influence. Be faithful. Take up your sacred burden reverently. Be sure that your heart is pure and that your life is sweet and clean.

J.R. Miller

❧

WHEN MY MOTHER TUCKED ME IN

Oh, the quaint and curious carving
On the posts of that old bed!
There were long-beacked, queer old griffins
Wearing crowns upon their head;
And they fiercely looked down on me
With a cold, sardonic grin;
I was not afraid of griffins
When my mother tucked me in.

What cared I for dismal shadows
Shifting up and down the floor,
Or the bleak and gruesome wind gusts
Beating 'gainst the close-shut door,
Or the rattling of the windows,
All the outside noise and din?
I was safe and warm and happy
When my mother tucked me in.

Sweet and soft her gentle fingers,
As they touched my sunburnt face;
Sweet to me the wafted odor
That enwrapped her dainty lace;
Then a pat or two at parting,
And a good-night kiss between;
All my troubles were forgotten
When my mother tucked me in.

Now the stricken years have borne me
Far away from love and home;
Ah! No mother leans above me
In the nights that go and come.
But it gives me peace and comfort,
When my heart is sore within,
Just to lie right still and, dreaming,
Think my mother tucked me in.

O the gentle, gentle breathing
To her dear hearts' softer beat,
And the quiet, quiet moving
Of her soft-shod, willing feet!
And, Time, one boon I ask thee,
Whatsoe'er may be my sin,
When I'm dying let me see her
As she used to tuck me in.

Betty Garland

The Author

Iwas in the company of a talented Christian lady when a friend said to her, "Why have you never written a book?"

"I am writing two," was the quiet reply. "Have been engaged on one for ten years, the other five."

"You surprise me," cried the friend, "what profound works they must be!"

"It doth not appear yet what they shall be," was her reply, "but when He makes up His jewels, my great ambition is to find them there."

"Your children?" I asked.

"Yes, my two children. They are my life work."

Christian Age

❧

No Secrets

The moment a girl has a secret from her mother, or has received a letter she dare not let her mother read, or has a friend that her mother does not know, she is in danger. A secret is not a good thing for a girl to have. The fewer secrets that lie in the hearts of women at any age, the better. It is almost a test of purity. She who has none of her own is best and happiest. In girlhood hide nothing from your mother. The girl who frankly says to her mother, "I have been there; met so and so; such and such remarks were made, and this or that was done," will be sure of receiving good advice and sympathy. If all was right no fault will be found. If the mother knows, out of her great experience, that something was improper or unsuitable, she will, if she is a good mother, kindly advise against its repetition. You may not know, girls, just what is right—just what is wrong, yet. You can't be

58

blamed for making little mistakes; but you will never do anything very wrong if from the first you have no secrets from your mother.

❧

I Had Eight Birds Hatcht in One Nest

I had eight birds hatcht in one nest,
Four Cocks were there, and Hens the rest.
I nurst them up with pain and care,
No cost nor labour did I spare
Till at the last they felt their wing,
Mounted the Trees and learned to sing.

Chief of the Brood then took his flight
To Regions far and left me quite.
My mournful chirps I after send
Till he return, or I do end.
Leave not thy nest, thy Dame and Sire,
Fly back and sing amidst this Quire.

My second bird did take her flight
And with her mate flew out of sight.
Southward they both their course did bend,
And Seasons twain they there did spend,
Till after blown by Southern gales
They Norward steer'd with filled sails.

A prettier bird was no where seen,
Along the Beach, among the treen.
I have a third of colour white
On whom I plac'd no small delight,
Coupled with mate loving and true,
Hath also bid her Dame adieu.
And where Aurora first appears,
She now hath percht to spend her years.

One to the Academy flew
To chat among that learned crew.
Ambition moves still in his breast
That he might chant above the rest,
Striving for more than to do well,
That nightingales he might excell.

My fifth, whose down is yet scarce gone,
Is 'mongst the shrubs and bushes flown
And as his wings increase in strength
On higher boughs he'll perch at length.
My other three still with me nest
Until they're grown, then as the rest,
Or here or there, they'll take their flight,
As is ordain'd, so shall they light.

If birds could weep, then would my tears
Let others know what are my fears
Lest this my brood some harm should catch
And be surpris'd for want of watch
Whilst pecking corn and void of care
They fall un'wares in Fowler's snare;

Or whilst on trees they sit and sing
Some untoward boy at them do fling,
Or whilst allur'd with bell and glass
The net be spread and caught, alas;
Or lest by Lime-twigs they be foil'd;
Or by some greedy hawks be spoil'd.

O would, my young, ye saw my breast
And knew what thoughts there sadly rest.
Great was my pain when I you bred,
Great was my care when I you fed.
Long did I keep you soft and warm
And with my wings kept off all harm.
My cares are more, and fears, than ever,
My throbs such now as 'fore were never.

Alas, my birds, you wisdom want
Of perils you are ignorant.
Oft times in grass, on trees, in flight,
Sore accidents on you may light.
O to your safety have an eye,
So happy may you live and die.
Mean while, my days in tunes I'll spend
Till my weak lays with me shall end.

In shady woods I'll sit and sing
And things that past, to mind I'll bring.
Once young and pleasant, as are you,
But former toys (no joys) adieu!
My age I will not once lament
But sing, my time so near is spent,
And from the top bough take my flight
Into a country beyond sight
Where old ones instantly grow young
And there with seraphims set song.

No seasons cold, nor storms they see
But spring lasts to eternity.
When each of you shall in your nest
Among your young ones take your rest,
In chirping languages oft them tell
You had a Dame that lov'd you well,
That did what could be done for young
And nurst you up till you were strong
And 'fore she once would let you fly
She shew'd you joy and misery,

Taught what was good, and what was ill,
What would save life, and what would kill.
Thus gone, amongst you I may live,
And dead, yet speak and counsel give.
Farewell, my birds, farewell, adieu,
I happy am, if well with you.

Anne Bradstreet

Praying Mothers ❧

MOTHER'S ELBOWS ON MY BED

I was but a youth and thoughtless,
    As all youths are apt to be;
Though I had a Christian mother
    Who had taught me carefully,
But there came a time when pleasure
    Of the world came to allure,
And I no more sought the guidance
    Of her love so good and pure.
Her tender admonitions fell
    But lightly on my ear,
And for the gentle warnings
    I felt an inward sneer.
How could I prove my manhood
    Were I not firm of will?
No threat of future evil
    Should all my pleasure kill.
But mother would not yield her boy
    To Satan's sinful sway,
And though I spurned her counsel
    She knew a better way.
No more she tried to caution
    Of ways she knew its pain.
And though I guessed her heartache
    I could not know its pain.
She made my room an altar,
    A place of secret prayer,
And there she took her burden
    And left it in His care.
And morning, noon and evening

By that humble bedside low,
She sought the aid of Him Who
   Best can understand a mother's woe.
And I went my way unheeding,
   Careless of the life I led,
Until one day I noticed
   Prints of elbows on my bed.
Then I saw that she had been there
   Praying for her wayward boy,
Who for love of worldly pleasure
   Would her peace of mind destroy.
While I wrestled with my conscience,
   Mother wrestled still in prayer,
Till that little room seemed hallowed
   Because so oft she met Him there.
With her God she held the fortress,
   And though not a word she said,
My stubborn heart was broken
   By those imprints on my bed.
Long the conflict raged within me,
   Sin against my mother's prayers.
Sin MUST YIELD for MOTHER NEVER
   While she daily met Him there.
And her constant love and patience
   Were like coals upon my head,
Together with the imprints
   Of her elbows on my bed.
Mother-love and God-love
   Are a combination rare,
And one that can't be beaten
   When sealed by earnest prayer.
And so at last the fight was won,
   And I to Christ was led,

And mother's prayers were answered
By her elbows on my bed.

Anonymous

ॐ

MOTHERS PUT YOUR CHILDREN TO BED

There may be some mothers who feel it to be a self-denial to leave their parlors, or firesides, or work, to put their children to bed. They think that the nurse could do just as well; that it is of no consequence who "hears the children say their prayers." Now, setting aside the pleasure of opening the little bed and tucking the darling up, there are really important reasons why the mother should not yield this privilege to any one. In the first place, it is the time of all times when a child is inclined to show its confidence and affection. All its little secrets come out with more truth and less restraints; its naughtiness through the day can be reproved and talked over with less excitement, and with the tenderness and calmness necessary to make a permanent impression. If the little one has shown a desire to do well and be obedient, its efforts and success can be acknowledged and commended in a manner that need not render it vain or self-satisfied.

We must make it a habit to talk to our children, in order to get from them an expression of their feelings. We cannot understand the character of these little beings committed to our care unless we do. And if we do not know what they are, we shall not be able to govern them wisely, or educate them as their different natures demand. Certainly it would be unwise to excite young children by too much conversation with them just before putting them to bed.

Every mother who carefully studies the temperament of her children will know how to manage them in this respect. But of this all mothers may be assured, that the last words at night are of great importance, even to the babies of the flock; the very tones of the voice they last listened to make an impression upon their sensitive organizations. Mothers, do not think the time and strength wasted, which you spend in reviewing the day with your little boy or girl; do not neglect to teach it how to pray, and pray for it in simple and earnest language, which it can understand. Soothe and quiet its little heart after the experiences of the day. It has had its disappointments and trials as well as its play and pleasures; it is ready to throw its arms around your neck, and take its good-night kiss.

Mother's Magazine

❧

When Mother Tucked Us In

No matter what our station,
   No matter where we roam,
At times our thoughts will wander
   To our dear childhood's home,
Life's earliest recollections
   Of one's own kith and kin.
Those days by love surrounded,
   When mother tucked us in.

Oh: Mother, glorious Mother!
   Although we loved you so,
In those glad days of childhood,
   Your worth we did not know;
How many life successes,
   And honours we may win,
Are due to early memories,
   When mother tucked us in.

Clara Simpson

❧

A MOTHER'S PRAYER

The sweetest sound heard through our earthly home,
The brightest ray that gleams from heaven's dome,
The loveliest flower that e'er from earth's breast rose,
That purest flame that, quivering, gleams and glows,
Are found alone, where kneels a mother mild,
With heart uplifted, praying for her child.

The stream of tears can never cease to flow
Long as life's sun shall shine on us below;
And many angels have been sent by God
To count the tear-drops wept upon life's road;
But of all the tears that glow, the least defiled
Are when a mother prays beside her child.

Because it is to mortal eyes unseen,
Ye call it foolishness, a childish dream,
In vain, ye cannot rob me of that thought,
That legend with such heavenly sweetness fraught,
That blessed angels have for ages smiled
To see a mother praying for her child.

Anonymous

❧

THE LITTLE BOY THOU GAVEST ME

Dear Lord, I bring to Thee my son
Whose tender years have scarce begun.
In this wee frame I know full well

A living soul has come to dwell
Who needs Thee now at childhood's gate,
Ere he shall grow to man's estate.
I covenant through hours apart
To pray for him with fervent heart,
To teach Thy Word with winsome voice
By day and night until his choice
Be but Thy blood for sin's deep stain,
And my small son is born again.
Then onward shall I pray the more
And teach Thy precepts o'er and o'er,
That he may grow, each boyhood hour,
By Thine indwelling risen power,
Lord, some small boys with none to care
Will never hear a mother's prayer;
Prepare my son with love aflame
To reach them with Thy saving name.
And make him, Lord, a polished tool,
A learner in Thy highest school.
A mother's part seems, oh, so frail!
But Thy strong arm can never fail.
To teach, to pray, to stand are mine;
Expectantly I yield to Thee
The little boy Thou gavest me.

Louise B. Eavey

My Mother's Prayer

As I wandered round the homestead,
    Many a dear, familiar spot
Brought within my recollection
    Scenes I'd seemingly forgot.
There the orchard meadow yonder,
    Here the deep, old-fashioned well,
With its old moss-covered bucket,
    Sent a thrill no tongue can tell.

Though the house was held by strangers,
    All remained the same within,
Just as when a child I rambled
    Up and down and out and in.
To the garret dark, ascending,
    Once a source of childish dread,
Peering through the misty cobwebs,
    Lo, I saw my trundle bed.

Quick, I drew it from the rubbish,
    Covered o'er with dust so long,
When, behold, I heard, in fancy,
    Strains of one familiar song,
Often sung by my dear mother
    To me in that trundle bed:
"Hush, my dear, lie still and slumber,
    Holy angels guard thy bed."

As I listened to the music,
    Stealing on in gentle strain,
I am carried back to childhood,
    I am now a child again.
'Tis the hour of my retiring,
    At the ducky eventide,
Near my trundle bed I'm kneeling,
    As of yore, by Mother's side.

Hands are on my head so loving,
    As they were in childhood's days;
I with weary tones am trying
    To repeat the words she says.
'Tis a prayer in language simple
    As a mother's lips can frame,
"Father, Thou who are in Heaven,
    Hallowed ever be Thy name."

Prayer is over, to my pillow,
    With a good-night kiss, I creep,
Scarcely waking while I whisper,
    "Now I lay me down to sleep."
Then my mother over me bending,
    Prays in earnest words but mild,
"Hear my prayer, O Heavenly Father,
    Bless, O bless, my precious child."

Yet I am but only dreaming,
    Ne'er I'll be a child again,
Many years has that dear mother
    In the quiet churchyard lain.
But the memory of her counsels
    O'er my path a light has spread,
Daily calling me to heaven,
    Even from my trundle bed.

T.C. O'Kane

❧

WHEN MOTHER PRAYED

I think that I shall never see,
This side of God's eternity,
A scene as lovely as the one
Which met my gaze when day was done,
In childhood years of long ago;

My mother sang, 'twas sweet and low,
Her face with love was all aglow,
She turned the pages of God's Word,
Her tender heart was deeply stirred.

She knelt, she prayed, oh, what a prayer!
I listened, lingering on the stair.
'God bless my boy'—I heard my name—
And there, within my heart, a flame
Began to burn, 'tis burning yet.
That hour I shall not forget!

Though mother dear no longer kneels
And prays for me, this night there steals
A ray of warmth into my heart.
And now, like her, from cares apart,
I pray, Her prayers still follow me—
A torch—and by its gleam I see
My home across the crystal sea.

David F. Nygren

NEVER FORGET TO PRAY

Never, my child, forget to pray,
Whate'er the business of the day:
If happy dreams have blessed thy sleep,
If startling fears have made thee weep,
With holy thoughts begin the day,
And ne'er, my child, forget to pray.

Pray Him by whom the birds are fed,
To give to thee thy daily bread:
If wealth his bounty should bestow,
Praise Him from whom all blessings flow:
If He who gave should take away,
O ne'er, my child, forget to pray.

The time will come when thou wilt miss
A father's and a mother's kiss;
And then, my child, perchance you'll see
Some who in prayer ne'er bend the knee:

From such examples turn away,
And ne'er, my child, forget to pray.

From Child's Book of Poetry

৯

CHILD'S SELF-EXAMINATION

Before in sleep I close my eyes,
These things I must remember thrice:
What I've been doing all the day—
What were my acts at work or play?
What have I heard, what have I seen?
What have I learnt where'er I've been?
What have I done that's worth the doing?
What have I done that I should not?
What duty was this day forgot?

Before in sleep I close my eyes,
These things I must remember thrice:
If I've done ill, then I must pray
That God would wash my sins away,
And for the merits of his Son,
Forgive the evil I have done;
Then, pardoned daily, filled with love,
I'll be prepared to dwell above,
And there, with angels round the throne,
The love of God for ever own.

Anonymous

Home Educating Mothers ❧

Two Temples

A Builder builded a temple,
He wrought it with grace and skill;
Pillars and groins and arches
All fashioned to work his will.
Men said, as they saw its beauty,
"It shall never know decay;
Great is thy skill, O Builder!
Thy fame shall endure for aye."

A Mother builded a temple
With loving and infinite care,
Planning each arch with patience,
Laying each stone with prayer.
None praised her unceasing efforts,
None knew of her wondrous plan,
For the temple the Mother builded
Was unseen by the eyes of man.

Gone is the Builder's temple,
Crumpled into the dust;
Low lies each stately pillar,
Food for consuming rust,
But the temple the Mother builded
Will last while ages roll,
For that beautiful unseen temple
Was a child's immortal soul.

Hattie Vose Hall

❧

THE READING MOTHER

I had a Mother who read to me
Saga of pirates who scoured the sea,
Cutlasses clenched in their yellow teeth,
"Blackbirds" stowed in the hold beneath.

I had a Mother who read my lays
Of ancient and gallant and golden days;
Stories of Marmion and Ivanhoe,
Which every boy has a right to know.

I had a Mother who read me tales
Of Gelert the hound of the hills of Wales,
True to his trust till his tragic death,
Faithfulness blent with his final breath.

I had a Mother who read me the things
That wholesome life to the boy heart brings—
Stories that stir with an upward touch,
Oh, that each mother of boys were such!

You may have tangible wealth untold;
Caskets of jewels and coffers of gold.
Richer than I you can never be—
I had a Mother who read to me.

Strickland Gillilan

❧

SOUL CULTURE

I said unto my gardener,
  "I want my vine to bear
The choicest, richest, largest grapes
  To be seen anywhere."
So he tied it here
And he cut it there,
  And he trained it along the wall
And, oh! The loveliest grapes appeared—
  The wonder of us all.

God said unto the mother,
  "I want your child to be
A godly, helpful, useful man—
  A messenger for Me."
So she curbed him here,
And she taught him there,
  And she urged him to what was right,
And o'er the heads of ill-trained sons,
  He towered in moral height.

H.E. Foster

GODLY DISCIPLINE

It is not to watch children with a suspicious eye, to frown at the merry outbursts of innocent hilarity, to suppress their joyous laughter, and to mould them into melancholy little models of octogenarian gravity. And when they have been in fault, it is not simply to punish them on account of the personal injury that you have chanced to suffer in consequence of their fault, while disobedience, unattended by inconvenience to yourself, passes without rebuke.

Nor is it to overwhelm the little culprit with angry words; to stun him with a deafening noise; to call him by hard names, which do not express his misdeeds; to load him with epithets which would be extravagant if applied to a fault of tenfold enormity; or to declare, with passionate vehemence, that he is the worst child in the world and destined for the gallows.

But it is to watch anxiously for the first risings of sin, and to repress them; to counteract the earliest workings of selfishness; to repress the first beginnings of rebellion against authority; to teach an implicit and unquestioning and cheerful obedience to the will of the parent, as the best preparation for a future allegiance to the requirements of the civil magistrate, and the laws of the great Ruler and Father in heaven.

It is to punish a fault because it is a fault, because it is sinful, and contrary to the command of God, without reference to whether it may not have been productive of immediate injury to the parent or others.

It is to reprove with calmness and composure, and not with angry irritation,—in a few words fitly chosen, and not with a torrent of abuse; to punish as often as you threaten, and to threaten only when you intend and can remember to perform; to say what you mean, and infallibly do as you say.

It is to govern your family as in the sight of Him who gave you authority, and who will reward your strict fidelity with such blessings as he bestowed on Abraham, or punish your criminal neglect with such curses as He visited on Eli.

Mother's Treasury

꙾

Your Duty

When little children try to shirk
From doing any honest work
And always have a good excuse
If asked to be of any use,
They'll find the lazy habit grow
As nearly all the elders know.
And very likely hard to break
Though one may lots of trouble take.
So, start today, and do your bit.
I'm sure you will be glad of it.

Fanny Allen

❧

Teaching the Bible to Children

The teaching of the Bible to children is, of course, a matter of especial interest to those of us who have families—and, incidentally, I wish to express my profound belief in large families. Older folks often fail to realize how readily a child will grasp a little askew something they do not take the trouble to explain. We cannot be too careful in seeing that the biblical learning is not merely an affair of rote, so that the child may understand what it is being taught. And, by the way, I earnestly hope that you will never make your children learn parts of the Bible as punishment. Do you not know families where this is done? For instance: "You have been a bad child—learn a chapter of Isaiah." And the child learns it as a disagreeable task, and in his mind that splendid and lofty poem and prophecy is forever after associated with an uncomfortable feeling of disgrace. I hope you will not make your children learn the Bible in that way, for you can devise no surer method of making a child revolt against all the wonderful beauty and truth of Holy Writ.

78

Probably there is not a mother here who could not, out of her own experience, give instance after instance of the queer twists that the little minds give to what seem to us perfectly simple sentences. Now, I would make a very strong plea for each of us to try and see that the child understands the simple and beautiful stories of the Bible; children understand readily the lessons taught therein; but I do think it necessary to see that they really have a clear idea of what each sentence means, what the words mean.

Probably some of my hearers remember the old Madison Square Presbyterian Church in New York when it was under the ministry of Dr. Adams, and those of you who remember the Doctor will, I think, agree with me that he was the adjective "saintly." I attended his church when I was a little boy. The good Doctor had a small grandson, and it was accidentally discovered that the little fellow felt a great terror of entering the church when it was vacant. After vain attempts to find out exactly what his reasons were, it happened late one afternoon that the Doctor went to the church with him on some errand. They walked down the aisle together, their steps echoing in the vacant building, the little boy clasping the Doctor's hand and gazing anxiously about. When they reached the pulpit he said, "Grandpa, where is the zeal?" "The what?" asked Dr. Adams. "The zeal," repeated the little boy; "why, don't you know, 'the zeal of thine house hath eaten me up?'" You can imagine the Doctor's astonishment when he found that this sentence had sunk deep into his little grandson's mind as a description of some terrific monster which haunted the inside of churches.

President Theodore Roosevelt

Be Your Child's Confidant

Always allow your child to tell you all that has happened to interest or annoy while absent from home. Never think anything which affects the happiness of your children too small a matter to claim your attention. Use every means in your power to win and retain their confidence. Do not rest satisfied without some account of each day's joys or sorrows. It is a source of great comfort to the innocent child to tell all its troubles to mother, and do you lend a willing ear. For know you, that as soon as they cease to tell you all these things, they have chosen other confidants, and therein lies the danger. O mother! This is the rock on which your son may be wrecked at last. I charge you to set a watch upon it. Be jealous of the first sign that he is not opening all his heart to you.

Anonymous

჻

CHILDREN'S SELF-DENIAL

At an early age children may be taught to forego little things, especially for the sake of others; for that shows a purpose. Afterwards they may be taught to bear disappointments and crosses as benefiting their own character, and preparing them for the heavier trials and sacrifices of mature age. It will help to self-conquest, if one distinct act of self-denial is practiced every day; and then it should be entirely voluntary and cheerful, for thus it is like fruit with the bloom on it; but when self-denial is grudging and complaining, it is indeed sour and acrid fruit.

Dulce Domum

჻

Lullaby Town

There's a quaint little place they call Lullaby Town—
It's just back of those hills where the sunsets go down.
Its streets are of silver, its buildings of gold,
And its palaces dazzling thing to behold;
There are dozens of spires, housing musical chimes;
Its people are folk from the Nursery Rimes,
And at night it's alight, like a garden of gleams,
With fairies, who bring the most wonderful dreams.

The Sandman is Mayor, and he rules like a King.
The climate's so balmy that, always, it's spring,
And it's never too cold, and it's never too hot,
And I'm told that there's nowhere a prettier spot;
All in and about it are giant old trees,
Filled with radiant birds that will sing when you please;
But the strange thing about it—this secret, pray, keep—
Is, it never awakes till the world is asleep.

So when night settles down, all its lights snap aglow,
And its streets fill with people who dance to and fro.
Mother Goose, Old King Cole and his fiddlers three,
Miss Muffet, Jack Sprat and his wife, scamper free,
With a whole host of others, a boisterous crew,
Not forgetting the Old Lady Who Lived in a Shoe
And her troublesome brood who, with brownie and sprite,
Go trooping the streets, a bewildering sight.

There's a peddler who carries, strapped high on his back,
A bundle. Now, guess what he has in that pack.
There's a crowd all about him a-buying his wares,
And they're grabbing his goods up in threes and in pairs.
No, he's not peddling jams nor delectable creams.
Would you know what he's selling? Just wonderful dreams!

There are dreams for a penny and dreams that cost two;
And there's no two alike, and they're sure to come true;
And the buyers fare off with a toss of the head,
And they visit the Sandman, then hie them to bed;
For there's nothing to do in this land of Bo-Peep,
But to frolic and sing and then go off to sleep!

John Irving Diller

Loyalty to Mothers ❧

AFTERWHILE

Afterwhile we have in view
The old Home to journey to;
Where the Mother is, and where
Her sweet welcome waits us there,
How we'll click the latch that locks
In the pinks and hollycocks,
And leap up the path once more
Where she waits us at the door,
How we'll greet the dear old smile
And the warm tears afterwhile.

James Whitcomb Riley

MOTHERS IN LOVING REMEMBRANCE

Each of us have now, or hold in loving remembrance, a glorious Mother. In our early youth Mother was all in all, but is it not a fact that as we grow older we become forgetful of her goodness and less thoughtful of the happiness we should be giving her in return for her tender devotion? This should not be a duty service, but one or purest love, and no matter how earnest are our efforts, we cannot repay her the joy and pleasure she gave us during our childhood days. Someone has forcefully said, "I would desire for a friend, the son who had never resisted the tears of his Mother," 'Tis only such sons that get the full sweetness out of life. Permanent success and happiness do not come as a reward of ingratitude, disrespect and lack of affection for Mother. The reverse has been, is now, and always will be true. The same old-fashioned, sweet Mother love must ever be the foundation for permanent, ideal home life. Without it the structure will fall and can never again be replaced.

Samuel Francis Woolard

જી

KISSED HIS MOTHER

She sat on the porch in the sunshine
As I went down the street—
A woman whose hair was silver,
But whose face was blossom sweet,
Making me think of a garden,
When, in spite of the frost and snow
Of bleak November weather,
Late, fragrant lilies blow.

I heard a footstep behind me,
And the sound of a merry laugh,
And I knew the heart it came from
Would be like a comforting staff
In the time and the hour of trouble,
Hopeful and brave and strong,
One of the hearts to lean on,
When we think all things go wrong.

I turned at the click of the gate-latch,
And met his many look;
A face like his gives me pleasure,
Like the page of a pleasant book.
It told of a steadfast purpose,
Of a brave and daring will;
A face with a promise in it,
That, God grant, the years fulfill.

He went up the pathway singing,
I saw the woman's eyes
Grow bright with a wordless welcome,
As the sunshine warms the skies.
"Back again, sweetheart mother,"
He cried, and bent to kiss
The loving face that was uplifted
For what some mothers miss.

That boy will do to depend on
I hold that this is true—
From lads in love with their mothers
Our bravest heroes grew.
Earth's grandest hearts have been loving hearts,
Since the time the earth began;
And the boy who kisses his mother
Is every inch a man!

Christian Intelligencer

☙

NOBODY KNOWS BUT MOTHER

How many buttons are missing today?
  Nobody knows but Mother.
How many playthings are strewn in her way?
  Nobody knows but Mother.
How many thimbles and spools has she missed?
How many burns on each fat little fist?
How many bumps to be cuddled and kissed?
  Nobody knows but Mother.

How many hats has she hunted today?
  Nobody knows but Mother.
Carelessly hiding themselves in the hay—
  Nobody knows but Mother.
How many handkerchiefs willfully strayed?
How many ribbons for each little maid?
How for her care can a mother be paid?
  Nobody knows but Mother.

How many muddy shoes all in a row?
  Nobody knows but Mother.
How many stockings to darn, do you know?
  Nobody knows but Mother.
How many little torn aprons to mend?
How many hours of toil must she spend?
What is the time when her day's work shall end?
  Nobody knows but Mother.

How many lunches for Tommy and Sam?
  Nobody knows but Mother.
Cookies and apples and blackberry jam—
  Nobody knows but Mother.
Nourishing dainties for every "sweet tooth,"
Toddling Dottie or dignified Ruth—
How much love sweetens the labor, forsooth?
  Nobody knows but Mother.

How many cares does a mother's heart know?
  Nobody knows but Mother.
How many joys from her mother love flow?
  Nobody knows but Mother.
How many prayers for each little white bed?
How many tears for her babes has she shed?
How many kisses for each curly head?
  Nobody knows but Mother.

Mary Morrison

FAITHFUL CHILDREN

And canst thou, mother, for a moment think
That we thy children, when old age shall shed
Its blanching honors on thy weary head,
Could from our best duties, ever shrink?
Sooner the sun from his high sphere should sink
Thank we, ungrateful, leave thee in that day
To pine in solitude thy life away,

Or shun thee, tottering on the grave's cold brink.
Banish the thought! Where'er our steps may roam
O'er smiling plains or wastes without a tree,
Still will fond memory point our hearts to thee,
And paint the pleasures of thy peaceful home;
While duty bids us all thy griefs assuage,
And smooth the pillow of thy sinking age.

Anonymous

୬

OUR TRUEST FRIEND

A mother is the truest friend we have, when trials, heavy and
sudden, fall upon us; when adversity takes the place of prosperity;
when friends who rejoice with us in our sunshine, desert us when
troubles thicken around us, still will she cling to us, and endeavor by
her kind precepts and counsels to dissipate the clouds of darkness, and
cause peace to return to our hearts.

Washington Irving

୬

To My Mother
"My Mother" (Matthew 12:48)

I love you Mother for your quiet grace,
For that dear smile upon your kindly face,
For marks of toil upon each loving hand,
That worked for me ere I could understand;
For all time's touches on your hair and brow,
For never were you quite so dear as now:
I will be loyal, faithful, loving, true,
For, Mother dear, I owe so much to you.

Clara Simpson

Mother Mine

O Mother mine, when I was small,
You seemed to me my all in all;
The sunshine shimmered in your face;
The flowers blossomed in your grace.
You laughed with me when I was gay
And kissed my childish tears away—
Mother dearie, Mother cheery, Mother mine.

O Mother, as the years rolled o'er
Our heads, I loved you more and more.
When weakness laid its hand on you
You were so patient, brave and true;
You seemed the sum of all things good;
My dream of perfect womanhood—
Mother dearie, Mother cheery, Mother mine.

O Mother mine, if I can be
To little ones who look to me,
A mother half as sweet and wise
And tender; if they but surmise
That in your likeness I have tried
To grow, I shall be satisfied,
Mother dearie, Mother cheery, mother mine.

Selected

My Mother

Who fed me from her gentle breast
And hushed me in her arms to rest,
And on my cheek sweet kisses prest?
   My mother.

When sleep forsook my open eye,
Who was it sung sweet lullaby
And rocked me that I should not cry?
   My mother.

Who sat and watched my infant head
When sleeping in my cradle bed,
And tears of sweet affection shed?
   My mother.

When pain and sickness made me cry,
Who gazed upon my heavy eye
And wept, for fear that I should die?
   My mother.

Who ran to help me when I fell
And would some pretty story tell,
Or kiss the part to make it well?
 My mother.

Who taught my infant lips to pray,
To love God's whole word and day,
And walk in wisdom's pleasant way?
 My mother.

And can I ever cease to be
Affectionate and kind to thee
Who wast so very kind to me,—
 My mother.

Oh no, the thought I cannot bear;
And if God please my life to spare
I hope I shall reward thy care,
 My mother.

When thou are feeble, old and gray,
My healthy arm shall be thy stay,
And I will soothe thy pains away,
 My mother.

And when I see thee hang thy head,
'Twill be my turn to watch thy bed,
And tears of sweet affection shed,—
 My mother.

Jane Taylor

FEMININITY
DEFENDED

And all the women that were wise hearted did spin with their hands.

EXODUS 35:25

A gracious woman retaineth honour: and strong men retain riches.

PROVERBS 11:16

A virtuous woman is a crown to her husband: but she that maketh ashamed is as rottenness in his bones.

PROVERBS 12:4

As a jewel of gold in a swine's snout, so is a fair woman which is without discretion.

PROVERBS 11:22

House and riches are the inheritance of fathers: and a prudent wife is from the LORD.

PROVERBS 19:14

It is better to dwell in the wilderness, than with a contentious and an angry woman.

PROVERBS 21:19

A continual dropping in a very rainy day and a contentious woman are alike.

PROVERBS 27:15

FEMININITY DEFENDED

Here is a startling revelation: Men and women are different! Even more startling to twenty-first century minds may be the fact that God intends us to rejoice in these differences. Men are to be masculine leaders and women are to be feminine helpmeets. We are to look different, to fulfill different roles, and to do so as if our lives depend on it—because they do. Upon the simple principle of distinction and authority rests all of law, society, and culture.

So why is this principle so hard for modern women? The answer is simple: We have bought a lie; a lie passed on for centuries from the first mother, Eve, and satanically cultivated through the modern feminist movement, the ultimate goal of which is the systematic annihilation of the Christian family. Feminism plays on the fears and insecurities of women, prodding us to reject the ancient doctrine of distinction and hierarchy in favor of androgyny and radical individualism.

Women, we must stop making apologies for God's creation order. We should give no quarter to ideas that will slay the happiness of our daughters and emasculate our sons. Let us speak the truth in love: It is wonderful to be a woman. It is glorious to be feminine. It is a privilege to do what no man can do: bring new life into this world. It is a joy and an honor to follow a godly man as his helpmeet, as together we serve the Lord. Hallelujah.

The American Legacy ❧

HOW THE AMERICANS UNDERSTAND THE EQUALITY OF THE SEXES

There are people in Europe who, confounding together the different characteristics of the sexes, would make man and woman into beings not only equal but alike. They would give to both the same functions, impose on both the same duties, and grant to both the same rights; they would mix them in all things—their occupations, their pleasures, their business. It may readily be conceived that by thus attempting to make one sex equal to the other, both are degraded, and from so preposterous a medley of the works of nature nothing could ever result but weak men and disorderly women.

It is not thus that the Americans understand that species of democratic equality which may be established between the sexes. They admit that as nature has appointed such wide differences between the physical and moral constitution of man and woman, her manifest design was to give a distinct employment to their various faculties; and they hold that improvement does not consist in making beings so dissimilar do pretty nearly the same things, but in causing each of them to fulfill their respective tasks in the best possible manner. The Americans have applied to the sexes the great principle of political economy which governs the manufacturers of our age, by carefully dividing the duties of man from those of woman in order that the great work of society may be the better carried on.

In no country has such constant care been taken as in America to trace two clearly distinct lines of action for the two sexes and to make them keep pace one with the other, but in two pathways that are always different. American women never manage the outward concerns of the family or conduct a business or take a part in political life; nor are they, on the other hand, ever compelled to perform the rough labor of the fields or to make any of those laborious efforts which demand the exertion of physical strength. No families are so poor as to form an exception to this rule. If, on the one hand, an American woman cannot escape from the quiet circle of domestic employments, she is never forced, on the other, to go beyond it. Hence it is that the women of America, who often exhibit a masculine strength of understanding and a manly energy, generally preserve great delicacy of personal appearance and always retain the manners of women although they sometimes show that they have the hearts and minds of men.

Nor have the Americans ever supposed that one consequence of democratic principles is the subversion of marital power or the confusion of the natural authorities in families. They hold that every association must have a head in order to accomplish its object, and that the natural head of the conjugal association is man. They do not therefore deny him the right of directing his partner, and they maintain that in the smaller association of husband and wife as well as in the great social community the object of democracy is to regulate and legalize the powers that are necessary, and not to subvert all power.

This opinion is not peculiar to one sex and contested by the other; I never observed that the women of America consider conjugal authority as a fortunate usurpation of their rights, or that they thought themselves degraded by submitting to it. It appeared to me, on the contrary, that they attach a sort of pride to the voluntary surrender of their own will and make it their boast to bend themselves to the yoke, not to shake it off. Such, at least, is the feeling expressed by the most virtuous of their sex; the others are silent; and in the United States it is not the practice for a guilty wife to clamor for the rights of women while she is trampling on her own holiest duties.

It has often been remarked that in Europe a certain degree of contempt lurks even in the flattery which men lavish upon women; although a European frequently affects to be the slave of woman, it may be seen that he never sincerely thinks her his equal. In the United States men seldom compliment women, but they daily show

95

how much they esteem them. They constantly display an entire confidence in the understanding of a wife and a profound respect for her freedom; they have decided that her mind is just as fitted as that of a man to discover the plain truth, and her heart as firm to embrace it; and they have never sought to place her virtue, any more than his, under the shelter of prejudice, ignorance, and fear. . . .

It is true that the Americans rarely lavish upon women those eager attentions which are commonly paid them in Europe, but their conduct to women always implies that they suppose them to be virtuous and refined; and such is the respect entertained for the moral freedom of the sex that in the presence of a woman the most guarded language is used lest her ear should be offended by an expression. In America a young unmarried woman may alone and without fear undertake a long journey.

The legislators of the United States, who have mitigated almost all the penalties of criminal law, still make rape a capital offense, and no crime is visited with more inexorable severity by public opinion. This may be accounted for; as the Americans can conceive nothing more precious than a woman's honor and nothing which ought so much to be respected as her independence, they hold that no punishment is too severe for the man who deprives her of them against her will. In France, where the same offense is visited with far milder penalties, it is frequently difficult to get a verdict from a jury against the prisoner. Is this a consequence of contempt of decency or contempt of women? I cannot but believe that it is a contempt of both.

Thus the Americans do not think that man and woman have either the duty or the right to perform the same offices, but they show an equal regard for both their respective parts; and though their lot is different, they consider both of them as beings of equal value. They do not give to the courage of woman the same form or the same direction as to that of man, but they never doubt her courage; and if they hold that man and his partner ought not always to exercise their intellect and understanding in the same manner, they at least believe the understanding of the one to be as sound as that of the other, and her intellect to be as clear. Thus, then, while they have allowed the social inferiority of woman to continue, they have done all they could to raise her morally and intellectually to the level of man; and in this respect they appear to me to have excellently understood the true principle of democratic improvement.

As for myself, I do not hesitate to avow that although the women of the United States are confined within the narrow circle of domestic life, and their situation is in some respects one of extreme dependence, I have nowhere seen woman occupying a loftier position; and if I were asked, now that I am drawing to the close of this work, in which I have spoken of so many important things done by the Americans, to what the singular prosperity and growing strength of that people ought mainly to be attributed, I should reply: To the superiority of their women.

Alexis de Tocqueville, Democracy in America

✿

Abigail Adams: Defender of Patriarchy

It is unfortunate that the fad in academic circles these days is to reinterpret the lives of the great ladies of our nation's past in light of the modern feminist paradigm. Such has been the case for Abigail Adams, devoted wife to our nation's second President.

We hear of Abigail the liberated woman, and of Abigail the feminist, but seldom do we here the truth about Abigail the submissive wife and keeper at home. Here was a brilliant woman who thoroughly embraced her role as helpmeet and homemaker. It is in her letters to her children and husband that we can best enjoy a glimpse of our former First Lady. A home educated woman with no "formal" education, Abigail had memorized huge portions of Shakespeare and Scripture, which she incorporated in her letters. That she was thoroughly conversant in the literature and culture of her day is also apparent. Her letters are quite simply works of art, which is what one would expect to see from the modern "liberated" woman, both in terms of their composition and content.

Writing to her ten-year-old son John Quincy, then traveling with his father, Abigail Adams would comment:

> You are in possession of a natural and good understanding and of spirits unbroken by adversity, and untamed with care. Improve your understanding for acquiring useful knowledge and virtue, such as will render you an ornament to society, an honor to your country, and a blessing to your parents . . . and remember you are accountable to your Maker for all your words and actions.

At a recent university lecture in my home town, the famed Adams historian, David McCullough, practically gushed as he described the influence and capabilities of Abigail as a stay-at-home mother. He praised her for home schooling her children and providing them with what was arguably the greatest education of their day—a parent-directed education superior to the best "schooling" offered today.

In God's providence, I had an opportunity to ask a question of the great author in the presence of a thousand person audience: "Professor McCullough, if Abigail were alive today and possessed the same worldview she espoused in the eighteenth century, would she align herself with modern feminism?" McCullough did not skip a beat, "No, she would have considered it her role as a woman to care for the home, raise the children, and support her husband."

So much for Abigail the feminist!

Selected from the Writings of Doug Phillips

᠉

CHIVALROUS BOY SCOUT

The same thing that entered into the training of these men, knights, pioneers . . . must enter into the training of the boy scouts of today. Just as they respected women and served them, so the tenderfoot and the scout must be polite and kind to women, not merely to well-dressed women, but to poorly dressed women; not merely to young women, but to old women: to women wherever they may be found—wherever they may be. To these a scout must always be courteous and helpful. When a scout is walking with a lady or a child, he should always walk on the outside of the sidewalk, so that he can better protect them against the jostling crowds. This rule is only altered when crossing the street, when the scout should get between the lady and the traffic, so as to shield her from accident or mud. Also in meeting a woman or child, a scout, as matter of course, should always make way for them even if he himself has to step off the sidewalk into the mud. When riding in a street car or train a scout should never allow a woman, an elderly person, or a child to stand, but will offer his seat; and when he does it he should do it cheerfully and with a smile.

1911 Boy Scout Handbook

❧

BOATS FOR WOMEN

"Votes for women!"
Was the cry,
Reaching upward
To the sky.
Crashing glass,
And flashing eye—
"Votes for women!"
Was the cry.

"Boats for women!"
Was the cry,
When the brave
Were come to die.
When the end
Was drawing nigh—
"Boats for women!"
Was the cry.

Life has many
Little jests
Insignificant
As tests.
Doubt and bitterness
Assail
But "Boats for women!"
Tells the tale.

St. Louis Post Dispatch

Wise Women ✖

KATE ON FOLLOWING HUSBANDS

Thy husband is thy lord, thy life, thy keeper,
Thy head, thy sovereign, one that cares for thee,
And for thy maintenance; commits his body
To painful labor, both by sea and land;
To watch the night in storms, the day in cold,
Whilst thou li'st warm at home, secure and safe;
And craves no other tribute at thy hands
But love, fair looks, and true obedience—
Too little payment for so great a debt.
Such duty as the subject owes the prince,
Even such a woman oweth to her husband;
And when she is froward, peevish, sullen, sour,
And no obedient to his honest will,
What is she but a foul contending rebel,
And graceless traitor to her loving lord?
I asham'd that women are so simple
'To offer war where they should kneel for peace,
Or seek for rule, supremacy, and sway,
When they are bound to serve, love, and obey.
Why are our bodies soft, and weak, and smooth,
Unapt to toil and trouble in the world,
But that our soft conditions, and our hearts,
Should well agree with our external parts?

Shakespeare's "The Taming of the Shrew"

✖

QUEEN VICTORIA ON "WOMEN'S RIGHTS"

I am most anxious to enlist everyone who can speak or write to join in checking this mad, wicked folly of "Women's Rights," with all its attendant horrors, on which her poor feeble sex is bent, forgetting every sense of womanly feelings and propriety. Feminists ought to get a good whipping. Were woman to "unsex" themselves by claiming equality with men, they would become the most hateful, heathen and disgusting of beings and would surely perish without male protection.

I love peace and quiet, I hate politics and turmoil. We women are not made for governing, and if we are good women, we must dislike these masculine occupations.

Queen Victoria, 1870

❧

A REMORSEFUL ACTRESS

I act for money, no other reason. Since I made my first picture in 1941, I haven't done a thing worthwhile. I have never enjoyed making films, and I don't like being a so-called film star. I haven't the emotional make-up for it, nor the love of exhibitionism. I am much too shy. [I'd rather find] one good man I could love and marry and cook for and make a home for, who would stick around for the rest of my life. I never found him. If I had, I would have traded my career in a minute.

Ava Gardner, arguably one of the most beautiful and talented women to grace the "silver screen," quoted in the Arizona Republic's *article on her death, January 27, 1990*

Feminism as Fraud ✣

THE PROPHESY OF ISAIAH CONCERNING FEMINISTS

As for my people, children are their oppressors, and women rule over them. O my people, they which lead thee cause thee to err, and destroy the way of thy paths. The LORD standeth up to plead, and standeth to judge the people. . .

Moreover the LORD saith, Because the daughters of Zion are haughty, and walk with stretched forth necks and wanton eyes, walking and mincing as they go, and making a tinkling with their feet: Therefore the LORD will smite with a scab the crown of the head of the daughters of Zion, and the LORD will discover their secret parts.

In that day the Lord will take away the bravery of their tinkling ornaments about their feet, and their cauls, and their round tires like the moon, The chains, and the bracelets, and the mufflers. The bonnets, and the ornaments of the legs, and the headbands, and the tablets, and the earrings, the rings, and nose jewels, the changeable suits of apparel, and the mantles, and the wimples, and the crisping pins, the glasses, and the fine linen, and the hoods, and the vails.

And it shall come to pass, that instead of sweet smell there shall be stink; and instead of a girdle a rent; and instead of well set hair baldness; and instead of a stomacher a girding of sackcloth; and burning instead of beauty. . .

And in that day seven women shall take hold of one man, saying, We will eat our own bread, and wear our own apparel: only let us be called by thy name, to take away our reproach.

Selections from Isaiah 3 and 4

✣

WHICH MISSION IS MOTHER'S?

She's a woman with a mission;
'Tis her heaven-born ambition
To reform the world's condition
    You will please to understand.

She's a model of propriety,
A leader of society,
And has a great variety
    Of remedies at hand.

Each a sovereign specific
With a title scientific,
For the cure of things morbific
    That vex the people sore.

For the swift alleviation
Of the evils of the nation
Is her fore-ordained vocation
    On this sublunary shore.

And while thus she's up and coming,
Always hurrying and humming,
And occasionally slumming,
    This reformer of renown:

Her neglected little Dicky,
Ragged, dirty, tough and tricky,
With his fingers soiled and sticky,
    Is the terror of the town.

Tid-bits

❧

Women's Rights Women

A recent incident on a railroad train justly illustrates the result [of women's "rights"]. A solitary female entered a car where every seat was occupied, and the conductor closed the door upon her and departed. She looked in vain for a seat, and at last appealed to an elderly man near her to know if he would not "surrender his seat to a lady." He, it seems, was somewhat a humorist, and answered: "I will surrender it cheerfully, Madam, as I always do, but will beg leave first to ask a civil question. Are you an advocate of the modern theory of women's rights?" Bridling up with intense energy, she replied, "Yes, sir, emphatically; I let you know that it is my glory to be devoted to that noble cause." "Very well, Madam," said he, "then the case is altered: You may stand up like the rest of us men, until you can get a seat for yourself." This was exact poetic justice; and it foreshadows precisely the fate of their unnatural pretensions. Men will treat them as they treat each other; it will be "every man for himself, and the devil take the hindmost." . . . [A]nd the society which will emerge from this experiment will present women in the position which she has always held among savages, that of domestic drudge to the stronger animal. . . . [S]he will reappear from this ill-starred competition defeated and despised, tolerated only to satiate the passion, to amuse the idleness, to do the drudgery, and to receive the curses and blows of her barbarized masters. . . .

[I]t would not be hard to show, did space permit, that this movement [women's suffrage] on the part of these women is as suicidal as it is mischievous. Its certain result will be the re-enslavement of women, not under the Scriptural bonds of marriage, but under the yoke of literal corporeal force. The woman who will calmly review the condition of her sex in other ages and countries will feel that her wisdom is to "let well enough alone. . . ." Under all other civilizations and all other religions than ours, woman has experienced this fate to the full; her condition has been that of a slave to the male—sometimes a petted slave, but yet a slave. In Christian and European society alone has she ever attained the place of man's social equal and received the homage and honor due from magnanimity to her sex and her feebleness. And her enviable lot among us has resulted from two causes: the Christian religion and the legislation founded upon it by feudal chivalry. How insane then is it for her to spurn these two bulwarks of defense. . . ? She is thus spurning the only protectors her sex has ever found, and provoking a contest in which she must inevitably be overwhelmed.

Robert L. Dabney, "Women's Rights Women"

ço

The Alternative to Submission is Exploitation

The alternative to submission is exploitation, not freedom, because there is no true freedom in anarchy. The purpose of submission is not to degrade women in marriage, nor to degrade men in society, but to bring to them their best prosperity and peace under God's order. In a world of authority, the submission of the wife is not in isolation, nor in a vacuum. It is set in a context of submission by men to authority; in such a world, men teach the principles of authority to their sons and daughters and work to instill in them the responsibilities of authority and obedience. In such a world, inter-dependence and service prevail. In a world of moral anarchy, there is neither submission to authority nor service, which is a form of submission. A husband and father who uses his authority and his income wisely to further the welfare of the entire family is serving the welfare of all thereby. But in a world which denies submission and authority, every man serves himself only and seeks to exploit all others. Men exploit women, and women exploit men.

R.J. Rushdoony, Institutes of Biblical Law

જી

THE MYTH OF MATRIARCHY

Do the women's liberationists want to be liberated from being women? No, they would say, they want to be liberated from society's stereotypes of what women are supposed to be. . . . Some very interesting facts have been uncovered by scientists which feminists will have to treat very gingerly for they show that it is not merely society which determines how the sexes will behave. . . . The idea of matriarchy is mythical, I've learned, for not one that can be documented has ever existed. Doesn't it seem strange that male dominance has been universal if it's purely social conditioning? One would expect to see at least a few examples of societies where women rather than men held the positions of highest status. . . . Isn't it really much easier to believe that the feelings of men and women throughout history bear a direct relationship to some innate prerequisite? . . . It was God who made us different, and He did it on purpose. Recent scientific research is illuminating, and as has happened before, corroborates ancient truth which mankind has always recognized. God created male and female, the male to call forth, to lead, initiate and rule, and the female to respond, follow, adapt, submit.

Elisabeth Elliot, Let Me Be a Woman

જી

Lost—A Boy!

Not kidnapped by bandits and hidden in a cave to weep and starve and raise a nation to frenzied searching. Were that the case, one hundred thousand men would rise to the rescue, if need be. Unfortunately the losing of this lad is without dramatic excitement, though very sad and very real.

The fact is his father lost him. Being too busy to sit with him at the fireside and answer his trivial questions during the years when fathers are the only great heroes of the boys, he let go his hold.

And his mother lost him. Being so much occupied with teas, dinners and club programmes, she let the maid hear the boy say his prayers, and thus her grip slipped and the boy was lost to his home.

Aye, the Church lost him. Being so occupied with sermons for the wise and elderly who pay the bills, and having good care for dignity, the ministers and elders were unmindful of the human feelings of the boy in the pew, and made no provision in sermon or song or personal contact for his boyishness. And so the Church and many sad-hearted parents are now looking earnestly for the lost boy.

Anonymous

Notable Quotes

Nor need we power or splendor,
Wide halls or lordly dome;
The good, the true, the tender—
These form the wealth of home.

Lucretia P. Hale

Hail, woman! Hail, thou faithful wife and mother,
The latest, choicest part of Heaven's great plan!
None fills thy peerless place at home; no other
Helpmeet is found for laboring, suffering man.

Rev. Mark Trafton

Persuading thousands of young mothers to go out to work and to abandon the care of their children to others is one of the most disastrous things at the present time. What is it going to profit the nation, if we gain the dollars—or even the whole world—but lose the souls of our children? Now that the State is lifting so much responsibility from parents, the bond of love between parents and their children is in danger of being loosened. It is when the mothers of the nation begin to fail in their duty to their children that religion disappears, moral standards fail, and the nation begins to go down.

Enid Blyton, discussing women in the military during WWI

Feminists who ceaselessly inveigh against their own oppression by men (often hardly specifying its exact nature) would ignore how they themselves have oppressed . . . feminine women. It oppresses a woman who could delight in domesticity to tell her that her domesticity makes her a parasitic inferior to men. It oppresses a woman who yearns to stay home with her children to tell her she is worthy only insofar as she achieves in the workplace.

F. Carolyn Graglia, A Brief Against Feminism

DAUGHTERS OF DESTINY

*Through faith also Sara herself received strength
to conceive seed, and was delivered of a child when
she was past age, because she judged him faithful
who had promised. . . . Women received their dead
raised to life again: and others were tortured, not
accepting deliverance; that they might obtain a
better resurrection: And others had trial of cruel
mockings and scourgings, yea, moreover of bonds and
imprisonment: They were stoned, they were sawn
asunder, were tempted, were slain with the sword: they
wandered about in sheepskins and goatskins; being
destitute, afflicted, tormented; (Of whom the world
was not worthy:) they wandered in deserts, and in
mountains, and in dens and caves of the earth. And
these all, having obtained a good report through faith,
received not the promise: God having provided some
better thing for us, that they without us should not be
made perfect.*

HEBREWS 11

*I commend unto you Phebe our sister, which is a
servant of the church which is at Cenchrea: That ye
receive her in the Lord, as becometh saints, and that
ye assist her in whatsoever business she hath need of
you: for she hath been a succourer of many, and of
myself also.*

ROMANS 16:1-2

DAUGHTERS OF DESTINY

Only to the modern mind is submission equated with weakness, femininity with simple-mindedness, and motherhood with unfulfillment. The Bible knows of no such dichotomy. The Scripture describes the virtuous and submissive woman as having "strength and honor," and being worthy of praise. She is neither a mouse, nor a pretty ornament.

The virtuous woman is a daughter of destiny. She thinks multi-generationally. She walks by faith in the light of the promises of God. These promises spur her on to live courageously and without compromise.

The daughter of destiny is precisely the type of woman described in the book of Hebrews. There we learn of the virtues of a former harlot named Rahab who stood alone against armies which defied Jehovah; we learn of Sara who heroically trusted in the promises of God even though they defied human experience; and we learn of the many faithful women, martyred for their beliefs, but unswerving in commitment to principle.

And so, we conclude this book of *Verses of Virtue* with a reminder that, like men, women are called to be heroic and noble and sacrifical. While it is not our role to die on foreign battlefields as soldiers, it is our role to live and die if necessary for the God we love and the vision He has proclaimed to us.

ESTHER SAVES A NATION

So the king and Haman came to banquet with Esther the queen. And the king said again unto Esther on the second day at the banquet of wine, What is thy petition, queen Esther? and it shall be granted thee: and what is thy request? and it shall be performed, even to the half of the kingdom.

Then Esther the queen answered and said, If I have found favour in thy sight, O king, and if it please the king, let my life be given me at my petition, and my people at my request: For we are sold, I and my people, to be destroyed, to be slain, and to perish. But if we had been sold for bondmen and bondwomen, I had held my tongue, although the enemy could not countervail the king's damage.

Then the king Ahasuerus answered and said unto Esther the queen, Who is he, and where is he, that durst presume in his heart to do so? And Esther said, The adversary and enemy is this wicked Haman. Then Haman was afraid before the king and the queen.

And the king arising from the banquet of wine in his wrath went into the palace garden: and Haman stood up to make request for his life to Esther the queen; for he saw that there was evil determined against him by the king.

Then the king returned out of the palace garden into the place of the banquet of wine; and Haman was fallen upon the bed whereon Esther was. Then said the king, Will he force the queen also before me in the house? As the word went out of king's mouth, they covered Haman's face.

And Harbonah, one of the chamberlains, said before the king, Behold also, the gallows fifty cubits high, which Haman had made for Mordecai, who spoken good for the king, standeth in the house of Haman. Then the king said, Hang him thereon.

So they hanged Haman on the gallows that he had prepared for Mordecai. Then was the king's wrath pacified.

On that day did the king Ahasuerus give the house of Haman the Jews' enemy unto Esther the queen. And Mordecai came before the king; for Esther had told what he was unto her. And the king took off his ring, which he had taken from Haman, and gave it unto Mordecai. And Esther set Mordecai over the house of Haman.

And Esther spake yet again before the king, and fell down at his feet, and besought him with tears to put away the mischief of Haman the Agagite, and his device that he had devised against the Jews.

Then the king held out the golden sceptre toward Esther. So Esther arose, and stood before the king, And said, If it please the king, and if I have favour in his sight, and the thing seem right before the king, and I be pleasing in his eyes, let it be written to reverse the letters devised by Haman the son of Hammedatha the Agagite, which he wrote to destroy the Jews which are in all the king's provinces: For how can I endure to see the evil that shall come unto my people? or how can I endure to see the destruction of my kindred?

Then the king Ahasuerus said unto Esther the queen and to Mordecai the Jew, Behold, I have given Esther the house of Haman, and him they have hanged upon the gallows, because he laid his hand upon the Jews. Write ye also for the Jews, as it liketh you, in the king's name, and seal it with the king's ring: for the writing which is written in the king's name, and sealed with the king's ring, may no man reverse.

Then were the king's scribes called at that time in the third month, that is, the month Sivan, on the three and twentieth day thereof; and it was written according to all that Mordecai commanded unto the Jews, and to the lieutenants, and the deputies and rulers of the provinces which are from India unto Ethiopia, an hundred twenty and seven provinces, unto every province according to the writing thereof, and unto every people after their language, and to the Jews according to their writing, and according to their language.

And he wrote in the king Ahasuerus' name, and sealed it with the king's ring, and sent letters by posts on horseback, and riders on mules, camels, and young dromedaries: Wherein the king granted the Jews which were in every city to gather themselves together, and to stand for their life, to destroy, to slay and to cause to perish, all the power of the people and province that would assault them, both little ones and women, and to take the spoil of them for a prey,

Upon one day in all the provinces of king Ahasuerus, namely, upon the thirteenth day of the twelfth month, which is the month Adar. The copy of the writing for a commandment to be given in every province was published unto all people, and that the Jews should be ready against that day to avenge themselves on their enemies. So the posts that rode upon mules and camels went out, being hastened and pressed on by the king's commandment. And the decree was given at Shushan the palace.

And Mordecai went out from the presence of the king in royal apparel of blue and white, and with a great crown of gold, and with a garment of fine linen and purple: and the city of Shushan rejoiced and was glad.

The Jews had light, and gladness, and joy, and honour. And in every province, and in every city, whithersoever the king's commandment and his decree came, the Jews had joy and gladness, a feast and a good day. And many of the people of the land became Jews; for the fear of the Jews fell upon them.

Selections from the Book of Esther

⁖

DAUGHTERS OF SARA

Likewise, ye wives, be in subjection to your own husbands; that, if any obey not the word, they also may without the word be won by the conversation of the wives; While they behold your chaste conversation coupled with fear. Whose adorning let it not be that outward adorning of plaiting the hair, and of wearing of gold, or of putting on of apparel; But let it be the hidden man of the heart, in that which is not corruptible, even the ornament of a meek and quiet spirit,

which is in the sight of God of great price. For after this manner
in the old time the holy women also, who trusted in God, adorned
themselves, being in subjection unto their own husbands: Even as
Sara obeyed Abraham, calling him lord: whose daughters ye are, as
long as ye do well, and are not afraid with any amazement.

1 Peter 3:1-6

❧

THE DAUGHTER OF DESTINY

Long before the present battle
   There was prophesied a day
Tinkling words, impov'rished prattle
   Itching ears to hearts would sway.

In that day of broken marriage.
   Femininity's demise,
Ladies lost their life and carriage.
   All were "smart," but none were wise.

Rose up Mistress Amazonia
   Warring woman lead with mirth.
Most forgot the Pauline proverb,
   "She'll be saved through childbirth."

Off to war went the daughters.
   Left behind the men and babes.
Noble womanhood was slaughtered.
   Craving freedom, became slaves.

Rise up Hannah—listen, hear it!
   Maidenhood's the royal throne,

Of those women, true of spirit,
   Loving heaven, hearth, and home.

Rise up Hannah—others follow.
   You will not proceed alone
And the victory's not hollow
   When the truth is set in stone.

From the ashes of a culture
   That knew God, but now knows none
Generations rose to prosper,
   Forged by light from His true Son.

Taught at home, but raised for warfare,
   Not the steel and fleshy kind,
But the battle that is more fair,
   When the Spirit girds the mind.

Now there stands a breed of woman
   Strong of mind, content of heart.
Cherishing the ancient virtues,
   And from them will not depart:

Love of truth, and love of mother;
   Purity; the Word of God;
Holiness to one another,
   Homes to build, and keep, and laud.

Rise up Hannah—here's God's token,
   That your youth has passed the test.
Three-fold strands will not be broken.
   In thy sisters' friendship rest.

Rise up Hannah—happy sister.
  Sarah's friend, Rebecca's love,
Sisters three, your God has given
  Tender hearts knit from above.

Stand they now this generation
  Birthed by hearts which turned to home;
Fathers who have changed direction
  Mothers who no longer roam.

And the future is a bright one,
  If to vision you will cleave
And will not trade God's truth for some
  Mess of pottage known as ease.

Prepare to hear the heathen grumble,
  Steel yourself to their complaint
Cynics moan and basely mumble
  Gnash their teeth, but they will faint.

They will faint, and will not follow
  For you tread the narrow road.
And its tread will chew and swallow
  Selfish seeds unjustly sewn.

In the end, the Lord will vanquish
  Vanquish them, but vindicate
All who love Christ's ancient order
  And enter in the narrow gate.

Rise up Hannah—faithful daughter.
  Onward Maiden to the quest.
You who called your mother blessed,
  Someday shall in kind be blessed.

Rise up Hannah—to your station!
Daughter fair of destiny.
Light the path for generations.
Raise the torch of liberty.

Douglas W. Phillips

১৯

Meeting "Daddy"

Sturdy and plump and clean and fair,
With big blue eyes and a tangle of hair,
There's a little lassie who runs to meet
Her father's step that rings on the street,
As, day after day, at the set of sun,
Father comes home when his work is done.

Making money for wife and weans,
Few are the sheaves the good man gleans;
All day long he is busy down-town,
Snowflakes sift where his hair was brown;
But he starts for home at an eager pace,
And love lights up the care-worn face.
For there at the window watching out
Is the little maid whose merry shout
Of "Daddy is here!" in his ear shall be,
Swift as he turns his own latch-key.
And glad is the heart at the set of sun
When father goes home with his day's work done.

Anonymous

১৯

BETSY'S BATTLE FLAG

From dusk till dawn the livelong night
She kept the tallow dips alight,
And fast her nimble fingers flew
To sew the stars upon the blue.
With weary eyes and aching head
She stitched the stripes of white and red,
And when the day came up the stair
Complete across a carven chair
  Hung Betsy's battle-flag.

Like shadows in the evening gray
The Continentals filed away,
With broken boots and ragged coats,
But hoarse defiance in their throats;
They bore the marks of want and cold,
And some were lame and some were old,
And some with wounds untended bled,
But floating bravely overhead
  Was Betsy's battle-flag.

Then fell the battle's leaden rain,
The soldier hushed his moans of pain
And raised his dying head to see
King George's troopers turn and flee.
Their charging column reeled and broke,
And vanished in the rolling smoke,
Before the glory of the stars,
The snowy stripes, and scarlet bars
  Of Betsy's battle-flag.

The simple stone of Betsy Ross
Is covered now with mould and moss,
But still her deathless banner flies,
And keeps the color of the skies.
A nation thrills, a nation bleeds,
A nation follows where it leads,
And every man is proud to yield
His life upon a crimson field
    For Betsy's battle-flag!

Minna Irving

❧

A Letter from Abigail to John Adams
June 18, 1775

Dearest Friend,

The Day; perhaps the decisive Day is come on which the fate
of America depends. My bursting Heart must find vent at my pen. I
have just heard that our dear Friend Dr. Warren is no more but fell
gloriously fighting for his Country—saying better to die honourably
in the field than ignominiously hang upon the Gallows. Great is
our Loss. He has distinguished himself in every engagement, by his
courage and fortitude, by animating the Soldiers & leading them on
by his own example—a particular account of these dreadful, but I
hope Glorious Days will be transmitted you, no doubt in the exactest
manner.

The race is not to the swift, nor the battle to the strong—but the
God of Israel is he that giveth strength & power unto his people. Trust
in him at all times, ye people, pour out your hearts before him. God is
a refuge for us.—Charlstown is laid in ashes. The Battle began upon

our intrenchments upon Bunkers Hill, a Saturday morning about 3
o'clock & has not ceased yet & tis now 3 o'clock Sabbeth afternoon.

'Tis expected they will come out over the Neck to night, &
a dreadful Battle must ensue Almighty God cover the heads of
our Country men, & be a shield to our Dear Friends. how [many
ha]ve fallen we know not—the constant roar of the cannon is
so [distre]ssing that we can not Eat Drink or Sleep—may we be
supported and sustain in the dreadful conflict. I shall tarry here till
tis thou[ght] unsafe by my Friends, & then I have secured myself a
retreat at your Brothers who has kindly offerd me part of his house.
I cannot compose myself to write any further at present—I will add
more as I hear further—

Tuesday afternoon—I have been so much agitated that I have not
been able to write since Sabbeth day. When I say that ten thousand
reports are passing vague & uncertain as the wind I believe I speak
the Truth. I am not able to give you any authentick account of last
Saturday, but you will not be destitute of intelligence—Coll: Palmer
has just sent me word that he has an opportunity of conveyance.
Incorrect as this scrawl will be, it shall go—I wrote you last Saturday
morning. In the afternoon I received your kind favar of the 2 june
and that you sent me by Captn. Beals at the same time,—I ardently
pray that you may be supported thro the arduous task you have before
you. I wish I could contradict the report of the Doctors Death, but it
is a lamentable Truth,—and the tears of multitudes pay tribute to his
memory—Those favorite lines [of] Collin continually sound [in my
Ears.]

> How sleep the Brave who sink to rest,
> By all their Countrys wishes blest?
> When Spring with dew'ey fingers cold
> Returns to deck their Hallowed mould
> She their shall Dress a sweeter Sod
> Than fancys feet has ever trod
> By fairy hands their knell is rung

By forms unseen their Dirge is sung
Their Honour comes a pilgrim grey
To bless the turf that wraps their Clay
And freedom shall a while repair
To dwell a weeping Hermit there—

I rejoice in the prospect of the plenty you inform me of, but
cannot say we have the same agreable view here. The Drought is very
severe, and things look but poorly.

Mr Rice & Thaxter unkle Quincy Col Quincy Mr Wibert all desire
to be rememberd, so do all our family. Nabby will write by the next
conveyance—

I must close, as the Deacon w[aits.] I have not pretended to be
perticuliar with regard to what I have heard, because I know you will
collect better intelligence—The Spirits of the people are very good.
The loss of Charlstown affects them no more than a Drop in the
Bucket,—I am

Most sincerely yours
Portia

ھ

The Mothers of the West

The Mothers of our Forest-Land!
   Stout-hearted dames were they;
With nerve to wield the battle-brand,
   And join the border-fray.
Our rough land had no braver,
   In its days of blood and strife—
Aye ready for severest toil,
   Aye free to peril life.

The Mothers of our Forest-Land!
   On old Kan-tuc-kee's soil,
How shared they, with each dauntless band,
   War's tempest and Life's toil!
They shrank not from the foeman—
   They quailed not in the fight—
But cheered their husbands through the day,
   And soothed them through the night.

The Mothers of our Forest-Land!
   Their bosoms pillowed men!
And proud were they by such to stand,
   In hammock, fort, or glen.
To load the sure old rifle—
   To run the leaden ball—
To watch a battling husband's place,
   And fill it should he fall.

The Mothers of our Forest-Land!
   Such were their daily deeds.
Their monument!—where does it stand?
   Their epitaph!—who reads?
No braver dames had Sparta,
   No nobler matrons Rome—
Yet who or lauds or honors them,
   E'en in their own green home!

The Mothers of our Forest-Land!
　　They sleep in unknown graves:
And had they borne and nursed a band
　　Of ingrates, or of slaves,
They had not been more neglected!
　　But their graves shall yet be found,
And their monuments dot here and there
　　"The Dark and Bloody Ground."

William D. Gallagher

Notes

Notes

Notes

N o t e s